The IT Project Management Answer Book

The IT Project Management Answer Book

David Pratt, PMP

MANAGEMENTCONCEPTSPRESS

MANAGEMENTCONCEPTSPRESS
8230 Leesburg Pike, Suite 800
Tysons Corner, VA 22182
(703) 790-9595
Fax: (703) 790-1371
www.managementconceptspress.com

Copyright © 2012 by Management Concepts, Inc.

All rights reserved. No part of this book may be reproduced or utilized in any form or by any means, electronic or mechanical, including photocopying, recording, or by an information storage and retrieval system, without permission in writing from the publisher, except for brief quotations in review articles.

Printed in the United States of America

Library of Congress Control Number
2012939568
978-1-56726-377-0

10   9   8   7   6   5   4   3   2   1

ABOUT THE AUTHOR

Dave Pratt, PMP, is a certified Project Management Professional with more than 20 years of experience in managing projects of all types and sizes. He has managed projects in both the public and private sectors, as well as in non-profit organizations and service clubs. He is the author of our *Pragmatic Project Management: Five Scalable Steps to Success* and more than 60 articles (as well as two novels).

Dave currently teaches project management at South Puget Sound Community College in Lacey, Washington. He led the curriculum design effort for that school's Project Management Certificate program, which was launched in October 2008.

He holds master's degrees in Management (Webster University) and Hospital Administration (Baylor University) and a BS in Psychology (Washington State University). He is a retired military officer and hospital administrator, and currently owns a successful consulting firm. He has taught marketing, health services management, and project management at the undergraduate and graduate student levels in the United States and China.

He frequently speaks at conferences on a variety of topics, including change management, leadership, innovation, and motivation. He is a member of numerous service and professional groups, including Lions Clubs International, the Project Management Institute, and the Military Officers Association of America.

CONTENTS

Preface xvii

Acknowledgments xix

CHAPTER 1: Why Projects Succeed 1

Success Factors 1

Q1 Why are IT projects considered so risky? 1

Q2 What are the key indicators of IT project success and failure? 2

Q3 How is business value defined in IT projects? 5

Q4 How do project cost, complexity, and risk affect how a project should be managed? 6

Project Management Considerations 7

Q1 Technical resources make the best IT project managers—right? 7

Q2 What approaches are available to help fill the qualified PM void? 8

Q3 Can anyone with project management experience manage an IT project? 8

Q4 What skills does an IT project manager need to be successful? 9

Q5 How do you determine the size of a project in order to scale your project management effort appropriately? 11

Types of IT Projects 12

Q1 What is the difference between an IT project and a business-oriented project? 12

Q2 What is a custom software development project? 12

Q3 What is a COTS package implementation project? 13

Q4	What is a software package integration project?	13
Q5	What is an infrastructure project?	13
Q6	What is a transfer system project?	13

CHAPTER 2: Organizing For Success 15

Project Organization 15

Q1	What constitutes an IT project's leadership team?	15
Q2	What is the Project Steering Committee?	16
Q3	What is a Project Advisory Group?	16
Q4	To whom should the IT project manager report?	16

Project Teams 18

Q1	What are the different types of resources included on an IT project team?	18
Q2	What skill sets are needed for the typical IT project team?	18
Q3	What are the roles and responsibilities of project team members?	18
Q4	What roles and responsibilities do vendors fill on project teams?	25
Q5	Where do the software developers fit into the project organization?	27
Q6	What is the role of the business analyst on the IT project team?	27
Q7	Who makes up the technical team for a project?	27
Q8	What are the qualifications for business team leader for an IT project?	28
Q9	What are the qualifications for a technical team leader for an IT project?	29
Q10	What are the qualifications for an implementation team leader?	29
Q11	Who is on the business team for an IT project?	29
Q12	How do project team organizations differ based on the types of IT projects?	30
Q13	How do you organize for custom software development projects?	32
Q14	How do you organize for COTS and transfer system projects?	32
Q15	How do you organize for system modernization projects?	32
Q16	How do you organize for infrastructure upgrade projects?	34

Q17	Is the quality assurance analyst a member of the project team?...........	36

Project Management Considerations 37

Q1	What is the role of the IT project manager?...	37
Q2	Who makes the best project manager—a technologist or a businessperson?...	37
Q3	Who handles test management?...	38
Q4	What is the role of the test manager?...	38
Q5	What is communications management?..	38
Q6	What is the role of the communications manager?...............................	39
Q7	What is a configuration manager?...	39
Q8	What is the role of a technical architect?...	39
Q9	What are SMEs, and what value do they provide to an IT project?....	41

CHAPTER 3: Project Initiation 43

Project Management Considerations 43

Q1	What tasks are carried out during the project initiation process?........	43
Q2	What skill sets are needed for an IT project team during project initiation?...	44
Q3	What is a vision statement?...	45
Q4	What role do project objectives play in an IT project?........................	46

Deliverables 48

Q1	What is a deliverable?...	48
Q2	What is a business case and why is it important?.................................	48
Q3	What is a feasibility study and why is it important during project initiation?...	50

The Project Charter 51

Q1	What is a project charter?...	51
Q2	What is included in an IT project charter?..	52
Q3	What deliverables are identified in the project charter?......................	53
Q4	Do you need detailed requirements before you can publish a project charter?..	54

CHAPTER 4: Project Planning 55

Project Management Considerations 55

- Q1 When does the project planning process begin for an IT project? 55
- Q2 Who designs a new IT system—the technical team, the business team, or the users? 57
- Q3 Is project planning different for different types of IT projects? 57
- Q4 What is Agile project delivery? 58
- Q5 How do you include users in the planning phase of an IT project? 62
- Q6 What is business architecture? 62
- Q7 What is a network architecture and what role does it play in IT project planning? 65
- Q8 What is data migration and how do you plan for it? 65
- Q9 How do you relate project status to a nontechnical project sponsor? .. 66
- Q10 What is requirements traceability and why is it important for IT projects? 67
- Q11 What role does business analysis have in the planning process? 69
- Q12 What risks should be considered when planning an IT project? 70

Deliverables 74

- Q1 What deliverables are typically generated during the project planning process? 74
- Q2 What level of detail do you need when identifying new system requirements? 75
- Q3 What is included in a project management plan for an IT project? 77

Test Planning 80

- Q1 What is unit testing? 80
- Q2 What is system testing? 80
- Q3 What is integration testing? 80
- Q4 What is performance testing? 81
- Q5 What is user acceptance testing? 81
- Q6 What is regression testing? 81

Q7	What documentation needs to be produced during and after testing?	82

Database Design 82

Q1	How do you organize database development during the planning phase?	82
Q2	What is database modeling?	83
Q3	What is a conceptual data model?	84
Q4	What is a logical data model?	85
Q5	What is a physical database?	85

CHAPTER 5: Project Execution 87

Project Management Considerations 87

Q1	When does project planning end and project execution begin?	87
Q2	Who leads the project execution effort?	88
Q3	What events are commonly tracked during the project execution process?	89
Q4	How frequently should the users be involved during execution of an IT project?	92
Q5	What is independent verification and validation?	92
Q6	Who should approve technical design documents?	93
Q7	What is project control and why is it important during the execution process?	94
Q8	How often should project team meetings be held?	95
Q9	What types of meetings are commonly held during IT projects?	96
Q10	What is configuration management?	98
Q11	What is change management and why is it important to IT projects?	98
Q12	What is a system readiness assessment?	99

Deliverables 102

Q1	What deliverables are developed during the execution process?	102
Q2	What comes first—the user manuals, the user acceptance testing, or the training?	104

Defect Management 104

Q1 What is the best way to manage defects, or bugs, during an IT project? 104

Q2 What is a defect log and what information does it contain? 106

Q3 Is it okay to abbreviate testing when the schedule is tight? 108

CHAPTER 6: Project Closeout 109

Project Management Considerations 109

Q1 When does project execution end and project closeout begin? 109

Q2 What are the typical activities undertaken during project closeout? 110

Q3 Who leads the project closeout process? 113

Q4 What is a project archive and why is it important? 113

Deliverables 114

Q1 How do you document successful completion of an IT project? 114

Q2 How do you confirm that the full scope has been delivered at project closeout? 114

CHAPTER 7: Project Monitoring and Control 119

Q1 What tools are used to monitor and control an IT project? 119

Q2 What is included in an IT project status report and why is it important? 121

Q3 How can a project manager manage a technical team when she lacks technical skills? 121

Q4 What is a code review? 123

Q5 What is an architectural test? 124

Q6 What is the best way to manage stakeholder expectations during an IT project? 124

Q7 How much control is too much control over a project team? 125

Q8 What is earned value analysis? 127

CHAPTER 8: Scope Management 129

Q1 How do you define the scope of an IT project? 129

Q2	How do you manage scope without squelching the project team's initiative?	130
Q3	What is scope optimization and why is it important to an IT project?	131
Q4	What deliverables are identified in a project's scope statement?	134
Q5	What is a use case and how does it relate to project scope?	134
Q6	Why is scope creep so common for IT projects?	134
Q7	What causes late-stage change requests that cost so much and slow projects down?	136
Q8	Who should approve change requests for an IT project?	137

CHAPTER 9: Time Management 139

Q1	What is the best way to develop a schedule for an IT project?	139
Q2	How do project schedules differ based on the type of IT project?	144
Q3	How does requirements traceability factor into development of a project schedule?	148
Q4	Who manages an IT project's schedule?	149
Q5	What common risks are associated with IT project scheduling?	149

CHAPTER 10: Cost Management 153

Q1	Why is cost management so difficult for IT projects?	153
Q2	What costs are typically associated with an IT project?	154
Q3	Who is responsible for tracking project costs for an IT project?	155
Q4	What information is contained in an IT project's budget/cost management plan?	156
Q5	What risks are commonly associated with cost management for IT projects?	157
Q6	What is the best way to manage contract resources on an IT project?	158

CHAPTER 11: Quality Management 159

Q1	What is quality and how do you plan for it?	159
Q2	How do you monitor quality during an IT project?	160

Q3	What tools are used to manage quality for an IT project?	161
Q4	How do you assess the quality of software developed for an IT project?	163
Q5	How do defects relate to an IT solution's quality?	164
Q6	What is the best way to manage defects found during an IT project?	164
Q7	Who defines quality for an IT project—the users or the technical team?	165
Q8	How do you convince a project sponsor to invest in quality when budgets are tight?	165

CHAPTER 12: Human Resource Management ... 167

Q1	How does human resource management relate to IT projects?	167
Q2	Who provides the business and technical resources for an IT project?	168
Q3	What is a fat project team versus a lean project team?	169
Q4	How do you gain the support of nontechnical SMEs working on technical projects?	171
Q5	How do you hold team members accountable when you don't share the same skill sets?	171

CHAPTER 13: Risk Management ... 173

Q1	What is risk management and how does it relate to IT project management?	173
Q2	What is included in a risk management plan for an IT project?	174
Q3	What risks are commonly faced by IT projects?	175
Q4	Who is the best person to manage risks for an IT project?	176
Q5	What tools are used to track and manage IT project risks?	176
Q6	How is risk management used to calculate contingency requirements for an IT project?	179

CHAPTER 14: Procurement Management ... 181

Q1	What is procurement management planning and why is it so important for IT projects?	181

Q2	Which comes first—the request for proposal or the procurement management plan?	182
Q3	Why do IT projects have so many contractors, who come and go, on the project team?	182
Q4	Is it okay for an outside contractor to manage an IT project for an organization?	182
Q5	How do you verify that your contractors have the skills they say they have?	183
Q6	What performance standards should be defined as part of a contract for IT services?	184

Bibliography 185

Index 187

PREFACE

Information technology (IT) projects are complex undertakings that require the best of any project manager and team if they are to be successful. That said, numerous IT projects are completed successfully every year. The difference between those successful projects and the ones that work out less favorably lies in the unique approaches and tools used by their project managers and teams.

The principles laid out in the Project Management Institute's *A Guide to the Project Management Body of Knowledge (PMBOK® Guide)*[1] go a long way in guiding any project toward success. Books like *The Project Management Answer Book*[2] and others help the project manager with specific suggestions regarding how to incorporate those standards into their own practice. Discard the tenets laid out in those tomes, and you do so at your own project's risk.

This book, *The IT Project Management Answer Book*, adds to and complements the knowledge laid down in currently available books on project management and does so from an IT perspective. It zeroes in on tools and approaches that can make IT projects successful. Read this book and apply the tools and approaches it contains, and your odds for success will increase accordingly.

This book provides a handy, topical reference in a question-and-answer format. It is organized around the standard project management processes and knowledge areas relied upon for all types of projects to ensure a common frame of reference. The pages of this book are meant to be thumbed through as questions arise on an IT project and dog-eared or marked up with a highlighter as you locate some piece of information that makes a difference for your IT project. The information provided in every chapter addresses questions that most IT project managers have asked at

---

[1] Project Management Institute, *Management Body of Knowledge (PMBOK® Guide)*, 4th ed. (Newtown Square, PA: Project Management Institute, Inc., 2008).

[2] Furman J., *The Project Management Answer Book* (Tysons Corner, VA: Management Concepts, Inc., 2011).

one time or another. The answers are framed in terms that anyone can relate to, regardless of the depth or lack of technical background.

The IT world seems to evolve and give birth to new terminology hourly. Standard terminology can be difficult to identify, making it hard to find common ground when discussing approaches and methodologies. When no term exists, IT professionals develop a new one on the fly. For those readers more technically inclined, the plain-speaking approach used in this book might provide a refreshing view of how the IT project management world is shaped. For those less technologically oriented (and there are many of us), this book describes the tools and solutions for dealing with IT's sometimes challenging quandaries in simple, straightforward terms.

It would have been nice to have a resource like *The IT Project Management Answer Book* over the past 20 or so years of project management, and it is time to fill that void. Good luck with your own IT project. I hope that you find this book a valuable resource and that all of your IT projects fulfill your sponsor's vision, provide value to your users, and thrill your project teams.

David Pratt, PMP
September 2012

ACKNOWLEDGMENTS

The people who made this book possible are legion. They include the technical team leaders, architects, business analysts, and project stakeholders with whom I have worked over the past 20-plus years. Sometimes they mentored me; occasionally, they frustrated me; always, they provided valuable lessons that stuck with me and made each successive project a little easier to manage. My thanks go out to each one of them. You cannot pay for that kind of education.

I mention a few of those individuals here because of the special impact they have had on my career and on my life. They have provided support, counsel, and long hours solving technical challenges and the world's most difficult problems. To Marcel Milat, Angel Pang, Mayank Desai, Rex Richardson, Larry Tenison, Debbie Spaulding, Gil Dean, and my many students from the Project Management Certificate Program at South Puget Sound Community College, I offer my heartfelt thanks.

My special thanks go out Myra Strauss, David Stockhoff, and the team at Management Concepts Press. They make the publication process an enlightening and enjoyable adventure. This book was vastly improved as a result of their patient and timely suggestions.

Chapter 1

WHY PROJECTS SUCCEED

IT projects are notoriously risky endeavors. When confronted with the prospect of a new IT project, business owners and executives too often predict dire outcomes: "If the project delivers anything at all, it will most likely be late and over budget."

That attitude seems a bit unfair, particularly when nearly one-third of IT projects meet their objectives, provide the full scope defined for the project, and do so on time and on budget. Even so, two out of three business owners and executives most likely share that perspective, because they sponsored the other two-thirds of the IT projects that struggled or failed.

So, what's the difference between a successful IT project and an unsuccessful one? What makes one seem so effortless and another a frustrating mess?

The following questions and answers are intended to provide you with some of the information you will need to hit the target for your IT projects.

SUCCESS FACTORS

Q1 Why are IT projects considered so risky?

In its truest form, IT project management is about creating something where nothing existed before. Sometimes we modify an existing system in a way that has not been attempted in the past. Every time we take on a project, we develop something that, to some greater or lesser degree, did not exist before. Venturing into the unknown requires experience and professional stamina.

Have you ever stepped into a dark room? You know you must negotiate your way through a maze of furniture. There is a light switch somewhere in the room to illuminate your way, if only you could find it. The absence of that illumination promises bumped shins and more.

Sometimes taking on a new IT project feels like stepping into a dark room. If you have not walked the paths that lead to IT project success before and have no source of illumination, the future can be very hard to see.

Experienced IT project managers bring knowledge of what lurks in the darkness of that room. They have tried, failed, tried again, and succeeded. They know where many of the switches to light the way to project success can be found. Unfortunately, there are not enough experienced, trained IT project managers to go around.

The presence or absence of a qualified project manager has been identified as a key indicator of project success or failure. If there is one reason why IT projects are so risky, it is that the supply of experienced, trained IT project managers remains so low.

Anyone can hang out a shingle and call himself a project manager. In organizations where IT project management is not a core competency, management appoints project managers because of their technical skills or business acumen, or because they are the only ones available to do the job. Little attention is paid to whether the person possesses the necessary credentials or background to handle the complexities of an IT project.

So, what is the answer? What do you do when you need a project manager for a risky IT project and there isn't one to be found?

The answer is to partner up. Sometimes that means pairing a good non-IT project manager with a good technical team leader who can supplement the project manager's lack of IT background. At other times it means matching an IT technical resource who might be the best candidate for project manager with a solid business resource who can relate to the project team members and translate the organization's needs into technical terms.

Q2 What are the key indicators of IT project success and failure?

Experience suggests that a handful of indicators can predict project success and can be relied upon. They include:

- *User involvement*—Relates to involving the right users, who will depend on the technical solution professionally and personally to meet their goals
- *Executive support*—Specifically related to how timely decisions are made regarding critical issues that impact the project
- *Clear business objectives*—The focus of the project must be on the business value that the project is to provide the organization, which is driven by a clearly articulated vision of the project's deliverable solution
- *Scope management*—Delivering what the users of the new system need to do their jobs; avoiding extraneous functionality that might never be touched by the users of the system

- *Business requirements management*—The ability to be flexible, yet decisive, in shaping, changing, and managing project requirements
- *Experienced project manager*—Having a project manager on the team who has experience with projects of similar size and complexity within the industry on which the project is focused
- *Financial management planning*—The presence of objective tools for monitoring and interpreting a project's financial status and relating that to project performance
- *Project team management*—Having access to project team members and subject matter experts with the requisite skills and knowledge to do the work necessary to provide an acceptable solution
- *Use of a formal methodology*—The availability of a project delivery approach that is formally identified yet executed as informally as possible
- *Project management tools and infrastructure*—The availability and application of tools to facilitate project success, such as schedules, collaboration tools, and scope management tools, and the ability to use and interpret the project artifacts produced by those tools
- *Procurement management planning*—Progressive and responsive procurement planning and execution processes that identify procurement needs and the best approach for filling those needs.

These indicators frequently form the bases of external quality assurance reviews of IT projects. A realistic assessment of whether the indicators are in place and show positive values reveals much about a project's chance of success. An assessment tool commonly used for this purpose is provided in Figure 1.1.

FIGURE 1.1 Project Success Assessment Matrix

Area Evaluated	Weight	Assessment	Score
User involvement—Engaging the "right" users, who have good communication skills and possess a realistic appreciation of the project management process	20	3	60
Executive support—The presence or absence of timely decision-making processes by senior management, as represented by the project sponsor	20	3	60
Clear business objectives—The project objectives must be clearly defined and understood throughout the project team and supported by the organization, and applied as a measure of correct project orientation	15	3	45

(continues)

(continued)

Area Evaluated	Weight	Assessment	Score
Scope optimization—Scope must be realistic and limited to those requirements necessary to meet the project sponsor's approved vision	15	3	45
Agile business requirements process—The ability to originate and manage requirements quickly and without major conflicts	10	3	30
Experienced project manager—Project managers possess technology and business background, good judgment and negotiation skills, and communication and organizational capabilities	10	3	30
Financial management—The project must be managed using good budget management practices	10	3	30
Project team management—The availability, involvement, and management of skilled resources with the necessary experience and expertise, when they are needed	10	3	30
Formal methodology—An appropriate, realistic, formal methodology that is implemented in as informal a manner as possible	10	3	30
Project tools—The development and use of standard project management tools for management and control of the project that are well understood and regularly used by the project team	15	3	45
Procurement management—The presence of proactive plans and processes for early identification, planning, and execution of acquisitions to support a project	15	3	45
TOTAL SCORE			450
WEIGHTED SCORE (450 max pts.)			100%

Assessment Rating Key: 0 = Not accomplished; 1 = Unsatisfactory; 2 = Marginally satisfactory; 3 = Satisfactory

The goal is to identify these success factors in advance, address them early in the planning process for any project, and develop a realistic estimation of a new IT project's ability to succeed. For ongoing projects, periodic assessment of the success factors and how they apply to the project can offer insight regarding how the project is progressing. Course corrections can then be made, if necessary, and focused on the area of the project most in need of attention.

Q3 How is business value defined in IT projects?

In project management parlance, an *objective* is defined as the business value provided to the organization. IT projects with well-defined business objectives relate well to the needs and concerns of the business owners who fund them.

From a practical perspective, IT project objectives are usually stated in SMART terms:

S—*Specific*. The focus of the objective should be on a single business value that relates to a core business strategy of importance to the organization.

M—*Measurable*. The business value should be quantifiable. The value should be stated in terms of percentage of increase or decrease, dollar value, or other measure. Note that "none" and "all" are quantifiable.

A—*Assignable*. One or more stakeholders in the organization should be willing to sign up as the sponsor for each specific objective developed for a project. If no one is willing to sponsor an objective, there is no practical reason for the organization to see the objective as valid. That objective would be considered out of scope.

R—*Realistic*. An objective should be reasonably achievable, given the constraints of money, time, available technology, and resources.

T—*Time-bound*. The business value identified by the objective should be achievable within a reasonable, defined period of time. Vague promises that things will get better over time by using a new technology are not enough to stimulate investment in something as risky as an IT project.

A good example of an objective for an IT project might be worded as follows:

> The new financial management system will cost approximately $1.5 million and deliver a savings of $500,000 per year through better management of aged accounts receivable, beginning one year after system implementation. The Finance and Accounting Department sponsors this objective, which can be satisfied using a readily available, off-the-shelf software package.

Note that the example business objective is specific, in that it is focused on financial management. Measures are provided in terms of cost and expected return within a specific period of time. A group of stakeholders has stepped forward to sponsor the objective, and it is achievable using existing, off-the-shelf technology. This is an excellent project objective in that a clear value will be delivered to the organization.

We use the term *IT project* to define a project that has a significant IT component. The term is a handy one that lets people know that completing the project will require specific skills—*IT* skills. However, a successful IT project in today's economically constrained world must provide a realistic, defined business value to the organization that sponsors and pays for the project. From that perspective, there is no such thing as a pure IT project. There are only business projects with heavy IT components.

Q4 How do project cost, complexity, and risk affect how a project should be managed?

IT projects come in all shapes and sizes. Some are so small that a project team can barely be put together before the project's timeline has passed. The project's cost is low; the project's complexity is low. The risk level of these projects produces little concern. Management of simple, straightforward efforts delivered like these is often based on the simple intuition of the project team members, and that can be enough.

The more a project ventures onto uncharted terrain, the more risk, cost, and complexity rise. It takes longer to conceive of, design, and construct the technical solution if it has not been done before. More management is required. These projects often require more sophisticated and costly resources, and they carry more risk due to their unique nature. As a result, there will be more to plan, control, and coordinate, and more project management will be required than would be needed for a much simpler, less risky project.

The scope of a project's needs is specifically related to the project's size, risk, and complexity. Figure 1.2 provides a graphic representation of the relationship between the size of a project and the level of effort required to manage it. For a small, simple project, do a little project management; for a larger, more complex, costly, and risky project, do more.

PROJECT MANAGEMENT CONSIDERATIONS

Q1 Technical resources make the best IT project managers—right?

Organizations often assume that the resident IT technical expert would be a natural to fill in as an IT project manager. That can be a bad assumption.

IT is a technical field, but project management is a people and leadership discipline. Technical resources typically enter the field to write code, work with hardware, build databases, and so on. They often lack the interest, soft skills, and project

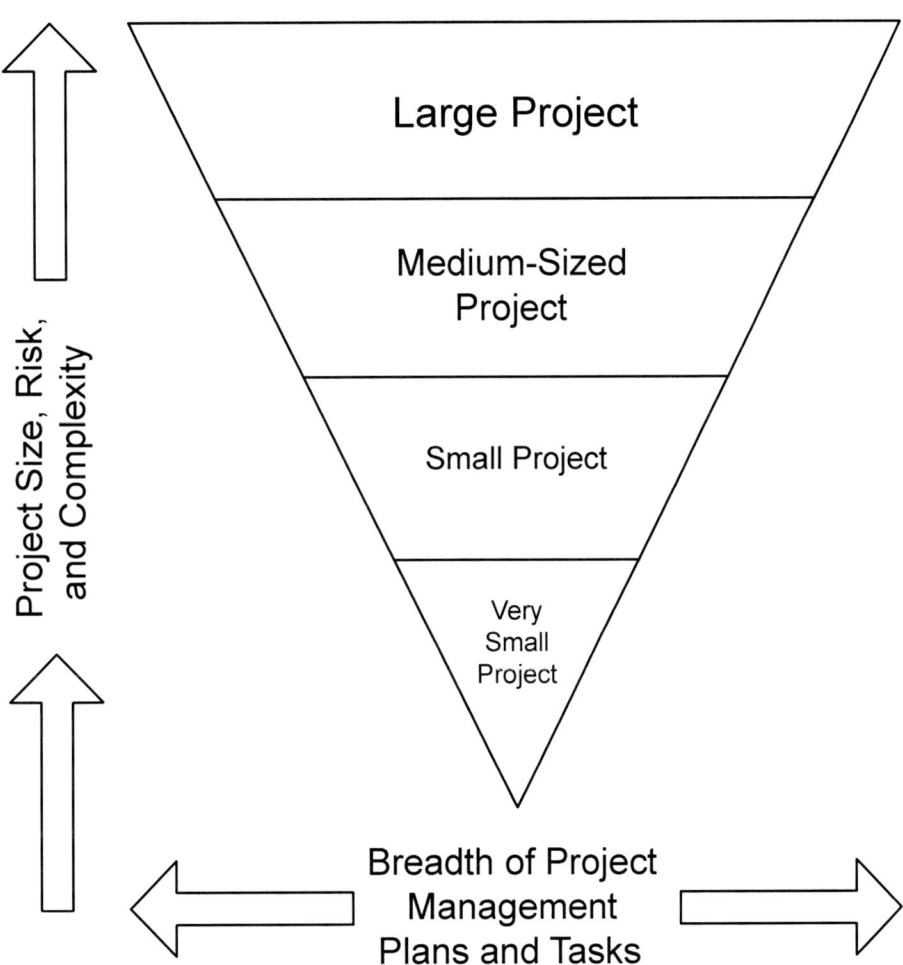

FIGURE 1.2 Project Scaling Model

management training necessary to manage a diverse team of technical and business staff.

It takes more than technical expertise to manage an IT project. In fact, many in the IT project management field believe there is no such thing as an IT project per se. They insist that IT projects are actually business projects, undertaken to fill a business need. Although the project might have a substantial IT component, the main emphasis of the project is to fill a business need.

The answer is to partner up. Sometimes that means pairing a good non-IT project manager with a good technical team leader who can supplement the project manager's lack of IT background. Other times, it means matching an IT technical resource who might be the best candidate for project manager with a solid business resource who can relate to the project team members and translate the organization's needs into technical terms.

Whenever possible, appoint the best person available to manage the IT project, not the person the organization can afford to lose from his regular job. Hopefully, this person will have the training needed to organize and control the project from beginning to end. If not, get the person the training, whether he is a technical or business resource. If the person lacks the background and expertise but remains your best prospect for managing the project, consider assigning a mentor who possesses the background and skills. Many project management consultants seek work of this sort, where they can offer their skills and knowledge to help inexperienced IT project managers learn, survive, and thrive.

Q2 What approaches are available to help fill the qualified PM void?

Project manager mentoring and Project Management Offices are two excellent mechanisms available to organizations that seek to increase their IT project management maturity but might lack the depth of skills needed to manage IT projects effectively.

Mentoring connections can take many forms. One option is to hire a highly-skilled IT project management consultant from outside the organization to guide and train the project manager. This service is often referred to as project management oversight. The consultant is generally available on a regular basis to work with the project manager, provide guidance and best practice suggestions, and help problem-solve unusual situations.

Q3 Can anyone with project management experience manage an IT project?

The simple answer to this question is "No."

It takes some appreciation of any industry to tune into the needs of a project. Consider one of the long-held thoughts about a project manager's role—to relate the project's vision and value to the project team. That person must have some appreciation of the industry in which an IT project is positioned to relate a project's value to anyone.

Purists will tell you that project management is project management, no matter the industry in which one is working. To some extent, they would be correct, but the technologies, processes, and goals vary considerably from industry to industry. There is no place where that is truer than projects that contain a large IT component—the ones we often refer to as IT projects.

With the prevalent shortage of qualified IT project managers, what is an industry to do when the only person available to manage a project lacks a significant technical background?

The answer, again, is partner up!

Find someone who has the technical background needed to translate tech-speak into terms the project manager can handle, and make that person the technical lead for the project. A team consisting of a qualified project manager and technical lead can take just about any IT project down the right road and increase that project's chance of success.

Q4 What skills does an IT project manager need to be successful?

First and foremost, the IT project manager needs an understanding of the IT discipline. Simply being a good technical resource is not usually enough to manage an IT project with an expansive, diverse project team membership.

For very small IT projects, a technical resource with some management experience might be well positioned to deliver a successful project. Good, straightforward management and task organization might be all that is required; i.e., set up a work plan, gather skilled resources, relate the goal of the effort to the resources, and get the work done.

For larger projects, where the risk is greater, the stakeholder community is more diverse, and the project team requires more and varied skill sets, a good manager with some IT skills might not be sufficient for the task. Something more is needed of the project manager. That something equates to:

- *Leadership*—The ability to get people to come together and do what they might not otherwise do on their own, and appreciate the value, the need of working together toward that common goal. No matter the challenge before them, if a good leader can bring a team together and relate to the value of reaching a goal, the team is more likely to embrace that goal regardless of the obstacles they might face.
- *Communications skills*—The demonstrated ability to listen; to speak, write, and organize thoughts rationally; and to relate those thoughts to a diverse group of individuals. Communications underpins the success or failure of every project, particularly when the number of stakeholders is great. The project manager must be a communications leader, even if a dedicated communications manager is assigned to the project.
- *Interpersonal skills*—The ability to relate to others with varied backgrounds, skills sets, and backgrounds, in a variety of stressful business, political, and socially dynamic situations. It is easy to organize resources and encourage them

toward a goal when things are going well. It takes real skill to relate to those same resources when they are in crisis, professionally or personally, and help them to get back on track and retain their place on the project team.

- *Experience with IT projects*—There is no replacement for experience. Good IT project managers bring a background of working in the IT industry, or at least some technical training to augment their business background. They relate to the technical staff in a manner that facilitates the interpretation of business requirements into technical terms that can be linked directly to how the solution should be constructed. Absent this experience, good IT project managers recognize the need to gather experienced technical resources around them, to complement their own skills.

- *Problem-solving skills*—Someone once said that a project is a problem scheduled for a solution. A good project manager can accurately define the problem statement that drives the project, identify potential solutions, direct the team toward the best alternative solution, and make that solution a reality.

- *Time management skills*—All projects work under time constraints. Managing to a schedule is fundamental to project management. Project managers must recognize these requirements and possess the ability to organize tasks and resources within time constraints.

- *Ability to develop people*—The ability to recognize the capabilities and limitations of team members, identify the gaps between the project's needs and the team members' abilities, and develop the team's membership to the point where the project can be successfully completed. The ability to accurately assess a team member's skills in a technical, business, or interpersonal area and then determine how to develop those skills in that team member is key to a project's success. Few teams assigned or hired for a project have all the tools they need to be successful. It is up to the project manager to identify and fill the gaps in the team's capabilities, using the resources available to the project.

- *Ability to handle stress*—Projects never seem to have enough time, money, or other resources to meet stakeholder expectations. This creates a lot of stress for the project manager. Effective IT project managers manage their own stress, recognize stress in others, and deal with it appropriately. It is essential that the IT project manager be perceived as the calm center of the storm during times when stress climbs to its peak. If the project manager appears ragged and out of sorts, the team loses confidence in that person and in their ability to function as a team. A critical item in the project manager's toolbox is effective techniques for anticipating, recognizing, and dealing effectively with stress.

IT project management is much more than technical skills or the ability to develop a project schedule using project management software. For an IT project manager to be successful, a professional toolbox that contains the skills described above is essential. The good news is that you can learn each skill by attending courses at training centers, community colleges, professional organizations, and so on.

Q5 How do you determine the size of a project in order to scale your project management effort appropriately?

Several dimensions can be used to assess the relative need for project management for any IT project. They are depicted in the table in Figure 1.3, which can be used as a guide when determining the depth of project management resources, processes, and bureaucracy to impose on any IT effort. As a point of reference, consider the column on the far right of the table, where a relative number of project management full-time equivalent positions are aligned with the relative size, complexity, risk, and cost of the project.

FIGURE 1.3 Project Scaling Guide

Project Description	Anticipated Dollar Value	Anticipated Complexity	Anticipated Level of Risk	Anticipated Impact	Project Management Requirement
Very small project	$25K to $50K	Few tasks	Low	1 department	Fraction of a PM
Small project	$50K to $100K	<100 tasks	Low	1 department	Fraction of a PM
Medium project	$100K to $1M	100 to 500 tasks	Low to high	>1 department	Dedicated, half-time PM
Large project	>$1M	More than 500 tasks	High	Many departments	Dedicated, full-time PM

Source: Pratt D., *Pragmatic Project Management: Five Scalable Steps to Success* (Tysons Corner, VA: Management Concepts, 2010), 9.

The concept of sizing project management efforts to fit the unique size, cost, complexity, and risk associated with a project is referred to as *scaling*. The goal of scaling a project is to provide the maximum benefit for the minimal investment of money and resources. Grasp this concept, and you can avoid the two traps so many fall into when they are confronted by an IT project with significant levels of risk, cost, and complexity:

1. Assuming that the project's risk and complexity are overstated and thus failing to implement adequate project management processes and procedures, or

2. Over-planning the IT project to the extent that the planning effort consumes excessive amounts of time, money, and other resources at the expense of the project's goals and objectives.

TYPES OF IT PROJECTS

Q1 What is the difference between an IT project and a business-oriented project?

The truth is there is no such thing as an IT project.

For many of us who work in the IT industry, suggesting that there is no such thing as an IT project comes close to blasphemy. IT projects are all around us. They abound in today's business world, where automated work processes and decision-support systems dominate the landscape. And while all this is true, it is equally true that the business need drives the demand for IT resources and not the other way around.

During the late 1990s and early 2000s, investment in IT projects was abundant. IT was the coming thing, and businesses looking for an edge wanted to be the first to have the next great automated tool to stimulate and support business opportunities. The investments made into IT during those years often focused on obtaining the latest technology for technology's sake, without the benefit of a clear vision of the value the technology would provide to the business.

IT projects felt like answers to questions no one had asked. When the project team delivered a solution, exactly how that solution applied to business remained unclear. Money was wasted. Investments were lost. Ultimately, an entire IT economy crashed in what is now referred to as the last days of the Dot Com Era.

In today's economically constrained economy, business value is the rule. For project sponsors to support a project, the project must provide a measurable benefit to the organization. A slick new technology, while of some interest to the IT purist, no longer provides sufficient return to justify any significant investment.

It is critical that IT project managers appreciate the need for their projects to provide a specific benefit to the sponsoring organization. The best way to conceive that benefit is to identify specific, clear project objectives that an IT project can deliver to an organization.

Q2 What is a custom software development project?

A custom software development project is one in which the project team intends to write the software to meet an organization's needs from scratch. The project team or vendors contracted for that purpose will develop all the software, databases, and so on. Of all the IT project types, this one carries the greatest risk of failure.

Q3 What is a COTS package implementation project?

For a commercial off-the-shelf (COTS) software package implementation project, the project team selects a predeveloped software package for support of an organization's business needs. COTS software packages are provided by software vendors as products that are purchased as fully complete and ready to use. Some COTS software packages give the project team the ability to configure certain, specific aspects of the software, within limits.

Though not risky to execute as a custom software development project, a COTS package implementation project often results in the need for a software vendor to customize the software package to meet the organization's specific requirements. If not managed closely, that need can grow to the extent that it might become more beneficial for the organization to develop its own software rather than implement the COTS package.

Q4 What is a software package integration project?

Software package integration projects take existing pieces of software and bring them together to support an organization's unique business needs. For example, a financial institution might have a preexisting finance and accounting system and desire to upgrade the accounts receivable piece of that system. The institution identifies a good COTS accounts receivable system and develops an IT project and a team whose job it is to integrate the legacy system with the new software package.

The risks associated with COTS software package implementation are similar to those where a software package is to be integrated with an existing system.

Q5 What is an infrastructure project?

Infrastructure projects implement or upgrade the capabilities of an organization to support the organization's technical systems. Such projects might include the replacement of hardware or the installation of new network switches or communications lines. Any project that affects the ability of systems to communicate within and outside an organization qualifies as an infrastructure project.

Infrastructure projects carry substantially less risk than software development and COTS package implementation projects, but they should be well planned just the same.

Q6 What is a transfer system project?

Transfer systems are systems that have been developed by one organization and are available for implementation for another organization with similar business needs.

The systems are not developed by commercial software houses and sold as COTS software packages but rather are developed for or by a specific organization to meet a particular need. That need might be duplicated in another organization and the software transferred to the other organization for its use. In the public sector, this sometimes happens at no cost to the receiving organization, although that is not always the case.

The level of risk associated with transfer system projects is equivalent to that associated with a COTS software package implementation project. Transfer systems often require more customization than anticipated once the IT project team assesses the system's capabilities and compares them to the receiving organization's unique needs.

Chapter 2

ORGANIZING FOR SUCCESS

People deliver projects. All the project management tools and techniques in the world won't deliver a successful project without the people to do the work. People take a project from the inkling of a good idea to an automated system or network that makes life easier and businesses more successful. Having the right people on the job, in the right positions and with clear expectations about their work, is a major step forward toward establishing a successful team—one that can provide a good outcome for any project. Organizing those resources in a meaningful, effective manner is a big step toward a successful project.

PROJECT ORGANIZATION

Q1 What constitutes an IT project's leadership team?

The only answer anyone can offer is, sadly, a tired and overused response: It depends. Every IT project is unique. It has its own technical requirements and business objectives that drive the skill set needs of the project and how those skill sets are organized.

No matter the type of project, however, someone always needs to be in charge. Someone will organize and manage the people. The project manager usually fills that role.

Someone other than the project manager owns the project. That person is responsible for writing checks (figuratively or literally) to pay for the effort and makes the hard decisions that can't be made at the project level. The project sponsor typically carries that burden.

Although the project sponsor and project manager are generally two different people, those roles are occasionally combined. For most successful projects, the project manager reports directly to the project sponsor (Figure 2.1). The balance of a project's organization springs from those two individuals and is shaped around the nature and specific needs of the effort.

FIGURE 2.1 Project Sponsor/Project Manager Relationship

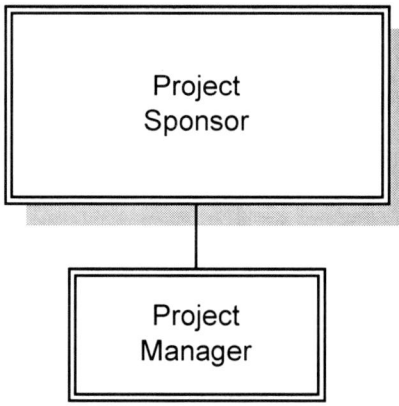

Q2 What is the Project Steering Committee?

Stakeholders who take a specific interest in a project can be a great asset. A *Project Steering Committee* is often organized as a vehicle for stakeholders who have a vested interest in the outcome of the project. The committee usually reports to the project sponsor, and although they don't have specific decision-making authority, they advise the project sponsor regarding important project requirements and organizational policy. They also serve as key communicators between the project and its public. This group is frequently referred to as the *Executive Steering Committee*. (The terms "Project Steering Committee" and "Executive Steering Committee" are interchangeable.)

Q3 What is a Project Advisory Group?

A *Project Advisory Group* is a subset of the Project Steering Committee and meets with the project sponsor to address specific issues raised during a project. The Advisory Group may consist of the director of information services, a senior business manager from the area to be supported by the new IT system, and the external quality assurance analyst. The group typically meets monthly and advises the project sponsor regarding issues that have been escalated to the project sponsor level by the project manager.

Q4 To whom should the IT project manager report?

Several years ago, a quality assurance analyst was called to a large state organization to assist with an IT project. The project had a 6- to 12-month schedule. The project's value was approximately $15,000,000. A vendor had been selected to provide the new system as an application service provider and had provided a beautiful proposal.

The project manager spent long hours answering emails, filing reports, and writing requirements for the project. He reported directly to the organization's IT director. The IT director did not manage the people who would ultimately own the system provided by the project, so those users had never met. The business manager for whom the users worked and the project manager had adjacent offices, but they did not talk.

The vendor informally reported to the business manager for contract guidance. The identity of the project's contracting officer was unknown. Together, the business manager and vendor instituted four major changes to the system's requirements specification without formal contractual documentation to authorize the changes.

There was no written project charter. No project plans existed, and there was no formal schedule or work plan. Over the first six months of the project, the vendor provided no project status reports. There was a requirements specification, but the vendor refused to accept or acknowledge that document. The vendor proposed immediate delivery of the new system.

The identity of the project sponsor remained a mystery to the project manager through the first six months of the project. The project was a mess.

The IT director was a smart woman. She recognized the condition of the project and that the business manager was free-wheeling changes to project scope. She saw that the project manager needed the support of someone who could hold all parties accountable and bring the project together before it was too late.

The quality assurance analyst was assigned to the project. He walked the halls of the agency's executive suite until he had identified the project sponsor. That person, a new senior manager in the organization, owned the business the new system would support and could make decisions regarding that business and the project. Everyone on the project, except the project manager, worked for that individual.

At the suggestion of the quality assurance analyst, the organization reassigned the project manager so that he reported directly to the executive. Six months later, with the project sponsor solidly in charge and supporting the project manager, the project was successfully delivered on schedule and within budget.

For the first six months of the project, it became apparent to the IT director that she could not make decisions that would stick or control the resources assigned to the project. The guidance she offered the project manager could not be acted on because those who constituted the project manager's team worked outside the IT director's purview. To get back on course, the project team needed a decisive person at the helm to support the project manager, bring the business manager under control, rein in the vendor, and get the project back on track.

To position a project manager effectively, she must work directly for the project sponsor. It is the project sponsor who can guide and support the project manager by making decisions that stick and committing the resources needed to complete the project's work.

PROJECT TEAMS

Q1 What are the different types of resources included on an IT project team?

Figure 2.2 illustrates one of the more common organization charts for IT projects. It is a good starting point for normalizing your own IT project's organizational structure. However, every project is different. Additional resources might be added to the project, based on a project's specific needs. You might come up with a new position or team structure that has never been used before, but as long as that new position or structure supports project success, it is impossible to be wrong.

Q2 What skill sets are needed for the typical IT project team?

The skill set requirements of each IT project are unique. That inherent aspect of an IT project is, perhaps, what makes such projects some of the most exciting and challenging projects in the project management field. For every project, a few new skill sets might be required, bringing people together in new ways.

The organization chart provided in Figure 2.3 lists many of the roles required for an IT project, by generic category. It also provides a good starting point for organizing those skill sets in a meaningful way.

Q3 What are the roles and responsibilities of project team members?

Although the specific skill sets within any role on an IT project vary with the business and technological nature of the project, many of the general roles and responsibilities remain constant across projects. Figure 2.4 provides an excellent list of project roles and responsibilities, many of which are unique to the IT project management discipline.

FIGURE 2.2 Typical IT Project Team Organization

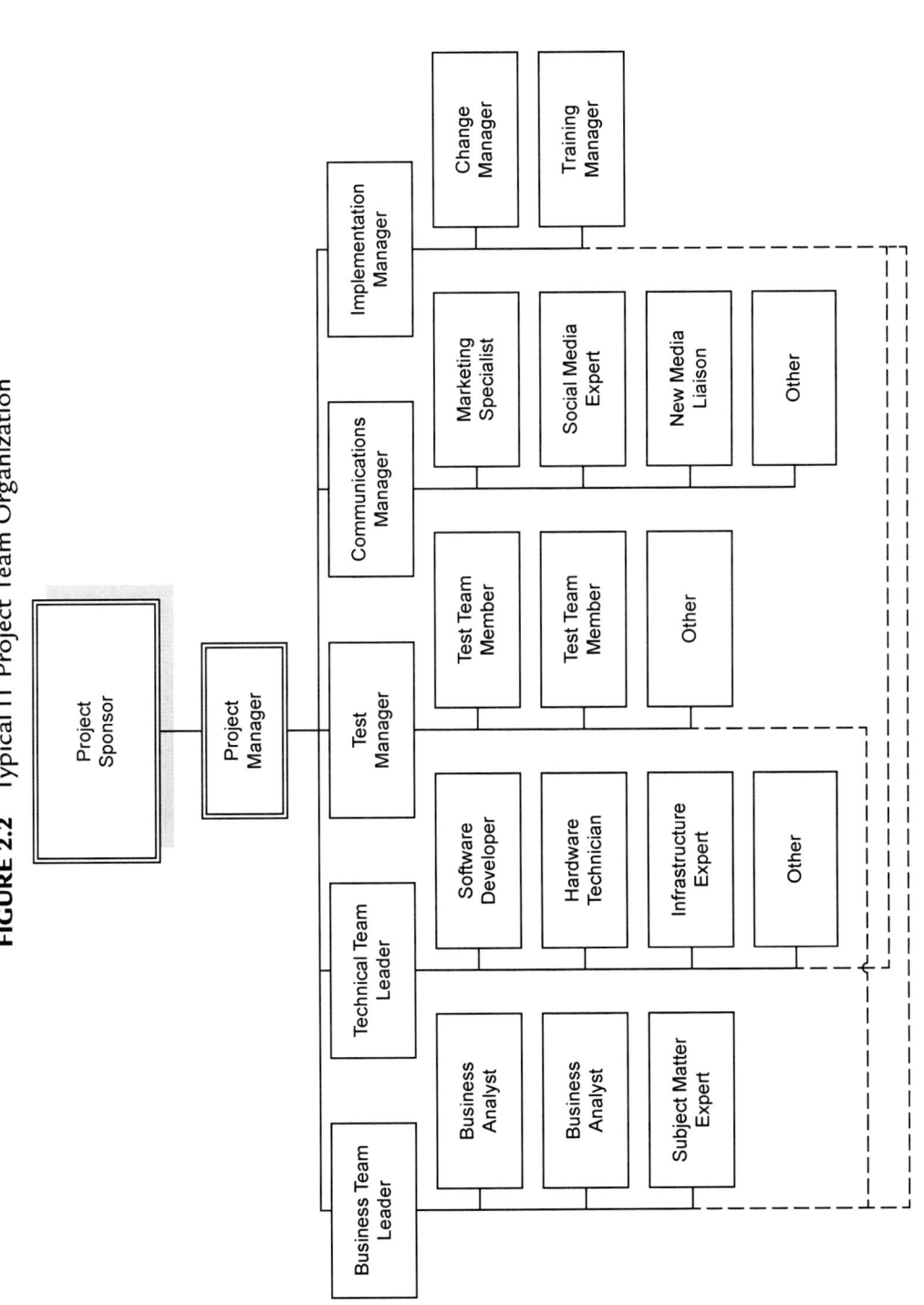

Note: Dotted lines between boxes indicate secondary reporting, occasional lines of communication, and informal relationships. Roles identified in a box with a dotted outline are not available on a full-time basis.

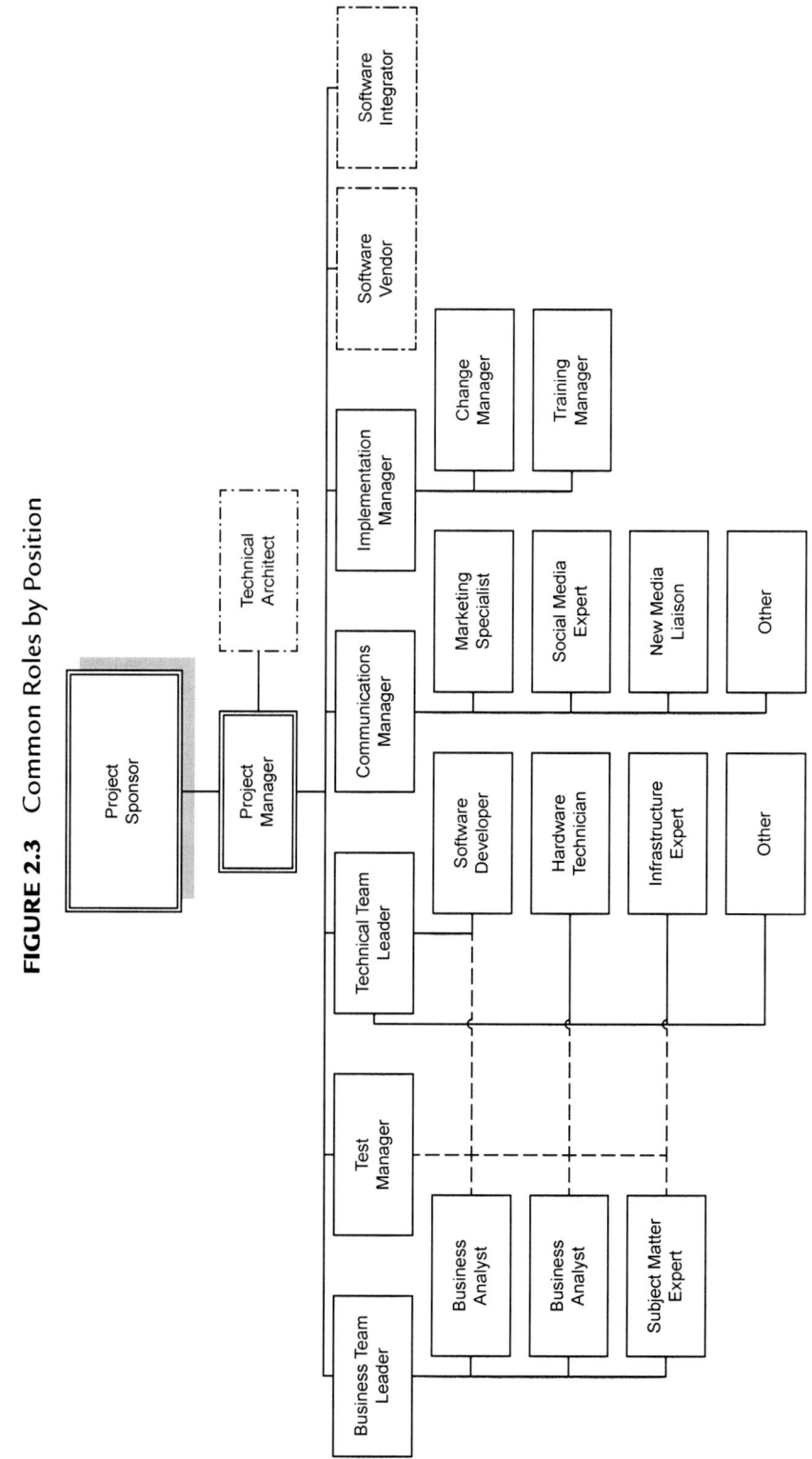

FIGURE 2.3 Common Roles by Position

FIGURE 2.4 IT Project Team Roles and Responsibilities

Owning Organization Roles	Responsibilities
Executive sponsor	• Act as final authority for escalated issues • Act as final authority on decisions related to the project budget
Project sponsor	• Business owner responsible for organizational, political, and financial support of the project • Defines the strategic vision, assists in project scope management, and conveys project importance to agency and external groups • Runs Steering Committee meetings • Resolves issues that cannot be resolved at a lower level • Provides budget accountability and contract signature authority • Drives policy decisions for the project • Communicates with key stakeholders, external entities, and partners • Authorizes supplemental personnel resources as required • Provides leadership as project champion • Approves scope, schedule, and budget changes
Project Steering Committee	• Reports to/advises the project sponsor • Advises the project sponsor regarding strategic vision and direction, including project scope • Assesses changes to agency policy as recommended by project management • Assists the project sponsor with priorities and resolving issues that cannot be resolved at a lower level • Communicates project status and outcomes to stakeholder groups (internal/external) • Escalates issues to sponsor(s) that cannot be resolved at this level • Makes project resources available
Project Advisory Group	• Reports to/advises the project sponsor • Provides input to Steering Committee and sponsors on project objectives, priorities, and requirements • Provides feedback to Steering Committee and sponsors on project direction • Communicates project progress and results to constituents

(continues)

(continued)

Owning Organization Roles	Responsibilities
External quality assurance	- Reviews project activities and project management processes - Reviews project deliverables - Provides the executive sponsor(s) with an independent assessment of project processes and products to ensure project objectives are realized - Regularly reports assessments, including project risks and recommended risk management strategies, to the project sponsor
Independent verification and validation (IV&V)	- Validates project functional and technical requirements from initial definition through implementation and reports on the outcome - Offers recommendations for course corrections
Project manager	- Reports to and takes direction from the project sponsor - Defines goals and objectives for the project consistent with executive decisions - Escalates issues to project sponsor that cannot be solved at a lower level and might impact timeframe, cost, or quality of the project - Manages the day-to-day tasks performed by the agency project team - Manages the deliverable review process to ensure the delivered solution meets the goals and objectives of the agency - Identifies risks and implements risk management strategies - Facilitates and promotes stakeholder communication - Monitors the deliverable and milestone schedule - Maintains project work plans, action item lists, and issue and risk logs for agency project team - Monitors and reports the overall project status, including the status of all vendor deliverables - Keeps the executive sponsor, project sponsor, and Steering Committee informed of project progress - Develops and manages statement of work documents - Determines project resource requirements and enlists stakeholder support to obtain these resources - Monitors and tracks project budget, schedule, and quality against defined project objectives - Oversees ongoing financial administration of the project - Ensures vendor contract compliance

Communications manager	• Oversees all internal and external communication activities • Develops and maintains the communications plan and documentation • Implements communications plan tasks and activities • Oversees management of project library
Change manager	• Facilitates changes to agency procedures, operations, and systems • Ensures that project activities are integrated and coordinated with other agency and organization initiatives and projects • Prepares the organization for project implementation
Training manager	• Manages training activities and deliverables, including the training plan, training curriculum, documentation, "train the trainers" activities, and scheduling of training sessions • Provides oversight for training staff activities • Reviews and approves vendor-supplied training materials and documentation
Business analyst lead	• Ensures the project supports stated user requirements • Develops interface requirements • Develops design documentation and specifications • Manages the business team
Business analyst	• Designs business process flows and specifications for the technical solution • Designs analytical views, key performance indicators, and dashboard requirements • Defines user roles and system access rights
Technical lead	• Manages technical staff responsible for implementing the functional requirements of the system, systems design, and verification activities • Coordinates definition of security profiles with users and implementation of those profiles with vendor • Participates in project team activities • Provides technical support during go-live • Coordinates the technical preparation of business operations for the application • Supports the development staff's technical requirements • Coordinates activities with external system owners to assist in resolving interface issues

(continues)

(continued)

Owning Organization Roles	Responsibilities
	• Coordinates data migration activities • Assists with the purchase of any software required to support the project • Configures system and ensures operational readiness for data migration, testing, training, production, etc. • Manages technical environment updates, security, and release management
Implementation manager	• Develops and executes implementation plan • Participates in project team meetings • Coordinates activities of agency and vendor project teams in accordance with duties defined by the project manager • Manages pilot and production rollout activities focusing on field implementation • Prepares implementation team resources to participate in implementation teams • Performs technical readiness assessment activities • Prepares the help desk and help desk personnel for supporting the solution
Test manager	• Coordinates test development and execution activities • Organizes people, facilities, and equipment needed for testing • Coordinates vendor preparation of test scripts with test team • Ensures traceability between the solution delivered by the vendor, defined system requirements, and test plans • Reviews vendor deliverables and reports for acceptance and defects • Manages resolution of testing issues • Tracks defects until resolved
Subject matter expert (SME)	• Represents the end user and business needs • Facilitates resolution of business and technical issues • Supports acceptance testing activities • Supports training activities • Reviews deliverables and provides feedback to ensure business needs are met • Supports definition of interface requirements and testing

	• Participates as "super user" during implementation planning
	• Assists in issue, risk, change, and problem identification, tracking, and resolution
	• Serves as an advocate for organizational change
SME trainer	• Develops training materials and curriculum for training workshops
	• Provides end user training sessions
	• Provides post-go-live support for users
SME tester	• Assists in testing processes and deliverables
	• Supports data migration, interface, and functional planning and testing

Q4 What roles and responsibilities do vendors fill on project teams?

Vendors provide many of the same functions as team members acquired from the project's sponsoring organization. They can act on the sponsoring organization's behalf in nearly every area of the project but should be limited from making decisions affecting organizational policy, budget, and project scope. They are transient resources. That lack of permanence within the organization makes them poor candidates for decision-making where the decisions last beyond their tenure.

Common roles and responsibilities filled by contract resources are listed in Figure 2.5.

FIGURE 2.5 IT Project Vendor Roles and Responsibilities

Vendor Roles	Responsibilities
Project manager	• Provides project leadership
	• Controls vendor project activities, providing leadership and direction
	• Establishes and oversees project management controls for issue, change, and risk management
	• Develops project plans and manages vendor project resources
	• Works cooperatively with agency team members to develop deliverables

(continues)

(continued)

Vendor Roles	Responsibilities
	• Participates in project team and project steering committee meetings • Coordinates activities of vendor project team • Manages vendor staff responsible for developing and implementing application solution • Manages and coordinates with agency staff project activities, including data conversion, systems interface development, test planning and execution, and go-live • Directs and oversees vendor staff responsible for monitoring and optimizing the performance of the system
Senior consultant	• Handles code change management (e.g., migration between development, testing, and production)
Consultant	• Works with SMEs to validate as-is business processes • Works with SMEs to design to-be business processes • Works with training manager to help develop training materials • Works with test manager to structure and manage testing efforts • Facilitates issue resolution
Senior business analyst	• Documents as-is business processes • Documents and designs to-be business processes • Helps facilitate testing • Helps facilitate training • Designs technical requirements for interfaces • Designs and develops analytical views, key performance indicators, and dashboard requirements
Developer	• Develops and configures solution that complies with stated user requirements and all other contract deliverables • Responds to defects until resolved
Trainer	• Directs and oversees vendor staff responsible for developing training strategies, programs, and support materials • Organizes and coordinates vendor-supplied training • Manages delivery of training for agency staff that will train and support end users • Schedules training

Q5 Where do the software developers fit into the project organization?

Software development represents the skill set most commonly associated with IT projects. Software developers write the code and implement the user interfaces that meet the project's requirements.

Software development tools evolve constantly. The challenge for the project manager is to hire skilled software developers who maintain a current knowledge of those tools and possess the skills needed for the project. If a technical architect is assigned to the project, that person can help the project manager interview software development candidates and administer hands-on tests of their skills to ensure their currency.

Q6 What is the role of the business analyst on the IT project team?

Business analysis as a skill set is not well understood or appreciated within the IT project management field. All too often, experts from the business are hired as business analysts, not realizing the need for the specific training required for them to be effective in the role.

A good business analyst has the ability to convert the organization's business processes into documentation that is actionable by the project's technical team. Not everyone experienced in a business makes a good business analyst. Although the person with 20 years in a field can provide valuable input to the project as a subject matter expert, he frequently lacks the detailed skills needed by a successful business analyst. Workflow diagrams, logical data models, user interface and report templates, and functional requirements specifications are the tools of the trade for a qualified business analyst.

Q7 Who makes up the technical team for a project?

IT projects have technical requirements that dictate the need for technically oriented resources. Data warehouse projects, Web site projects, business intelligence projects, workflow projects, and other types of IT projects require skilled resources to ensure project success. This need necessitates the addition of a technical team component to the IT project team structure. When the technical team has many members, a team leader should be assigned to help the project manager direct and control team member efforts.

Q8 What are the qualifications for business team leader for an IT project?

IT projects commonly have at least two team leaders if they have any at all—a technical team leader and a business team leader. There can be other team leaders on large projects, such as communications manager, test manager, and implementation team leader (Figure 2.6). Any one of these individuals may supervise and direct the efforts of many project team members.

FIGURE 2.6—PROJECT TEAM LEADERS

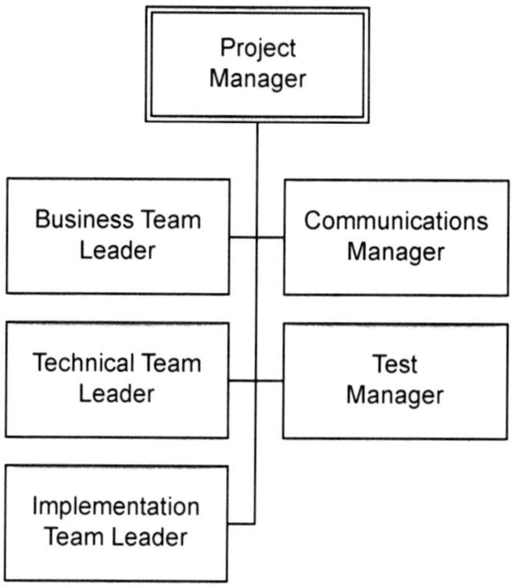

```
                    ┌─────────────┐
                    │   Project   │
                    │   Manager   │
                    └──────┬──────┘
         ┌─────────────────┼─────────────────┐
┌─────────────────┐                 ┌─────────────────┐
│  Business Team  │─────────────────│  Communications │
│     Leader      │                 │     Manager     │
└─────────────────┘                 └─────────────────┘
┌─────────────────┐                 ┌─────────────────┐
│  Technical Team │─────────────────│      Test       │
│     Leader      │                 │     Manager     │
└─────────────────┘                 └─────────────────┘
┌─────────────────┐
│  Implementation │
│   Team Leader   │
└─────────────────┘
```

A business team leader should be someone with a good background in business analysis. The person must have good communication and interpersonal skills. The business team leader will interview system users to identify detailed project requirements.

The business team leader will manage and direct the members of the team. Experience with managing teams of people on similar types of projects would provide excellent background for a business team leader on a complex IT project.

The business team leader should have experience in developing system requirements specifications, workflow diagrams, use cases, and other business-oriented project artifacts. Additional beneficial skills include a basic understanding of data modeling, report template development, cost analysis, and the industry in which the project is situated.

Q9 What are the qualifications for a technical team leader for an IT project?

The technical team leader must also be a good communicator. This person works with other members of the project management team and should be a skilled listener, writer, and speaker. The technical team leader should have experience organizing and managing resources. He should be the project's expert on the technology on which the IT project is focused.

The technical team leader should have experience with interpreting system requirements specifications, workflow diagrams, use cases, and other business-oriented project artifacts to guide the technical team in the construction of the project's technical solution. Additional beneficial skills include database design, software development tools, and test management.

Q10 What are the qualifications for an implementation team leader?

The implementation team leader should be highly organized. This person's communications must be excellent, and she should possess an excellent knowledge of the organization into which the new technical solution is to be deployed.

The implementation team leader ensures that system users have been trained to use the technical solution and works with the communications manager to ensure that the business is prepared for the changes that the new technical solution will stimulate within the organization. The implementation team leader will coordinate with the test manager, training manager, maintenance team, document manager, and technical team to develop detailed plans for moving the project's technical solution from development into the production environment.

Q11 Who is on the business team for an IT project?

IT projects exist for one reason—to support the business needs of the organization. From that standpoint, it is essential that the business side of the organization be represented on the project team. The roles of those team members come in the form of the subject matter expert (SME) and the business analyst. Business analysts and SMEs commonly organize into a business team for ease of management and communications. When this team has many members, a business team leader is assigned to assist the project manager in making team assignments and overseeing team member efforts.

SMEs bring specific experience and knowledge of the business to the IT project. Their input is critical to the success of the project. They can answer questions about specific functionality that is required for the technical solution, the configuration of reports, and how users are likely to interface with the new solution. SMEs are generally not full-time members of the project team but come and go as needed, when called upon by team members.

Business analysts are the team members who directly translate the organization's business needs into a language that can be understood and used by the technical team to construct and configure the technical solution. It is the business analyst who develops the detailed requirements lists, functional specifications, use cases, and other critical artifacts that are the blueprints defining exactly how the technical solution should be constructed. With help from the SMEs, business analysts become the business experts who will sit side-by-side with the technical team to identify exactly what must be developed.

Q12 How do project team organizations differ based on the types of IT projects?

The overall structure of an IT project's team generally remains constant from project to project. Figure 2.7 depicts a typical organizational structure for an IT project of some size and complexity.

It is the depth of resource requirements for any project that can vary substantially. Consider the common types of IT projects ongoing at any time in any industry:

- *Custom software development*—Software is written from scratch and implemented as a new system.
- *Commercial, off-the-shelf (COTS) implementation*—A software package is purchased and deployed to support a business need.
- *System modernization*—A system is upgraded to leverage new technology.
- *Transfer system*—A system is purchased from another organization that had similar needs and customized its own solution.
- *COTS integration*—A software package is integrated with an existing system or as part of a customized technical solution.
- *Infrastructure upgrade*—An organization's hardware, network, and so on are upgraded to support new or expanding technology.

Each type of project requires a slightly different depth of skill sets, particularly in the technical fields.

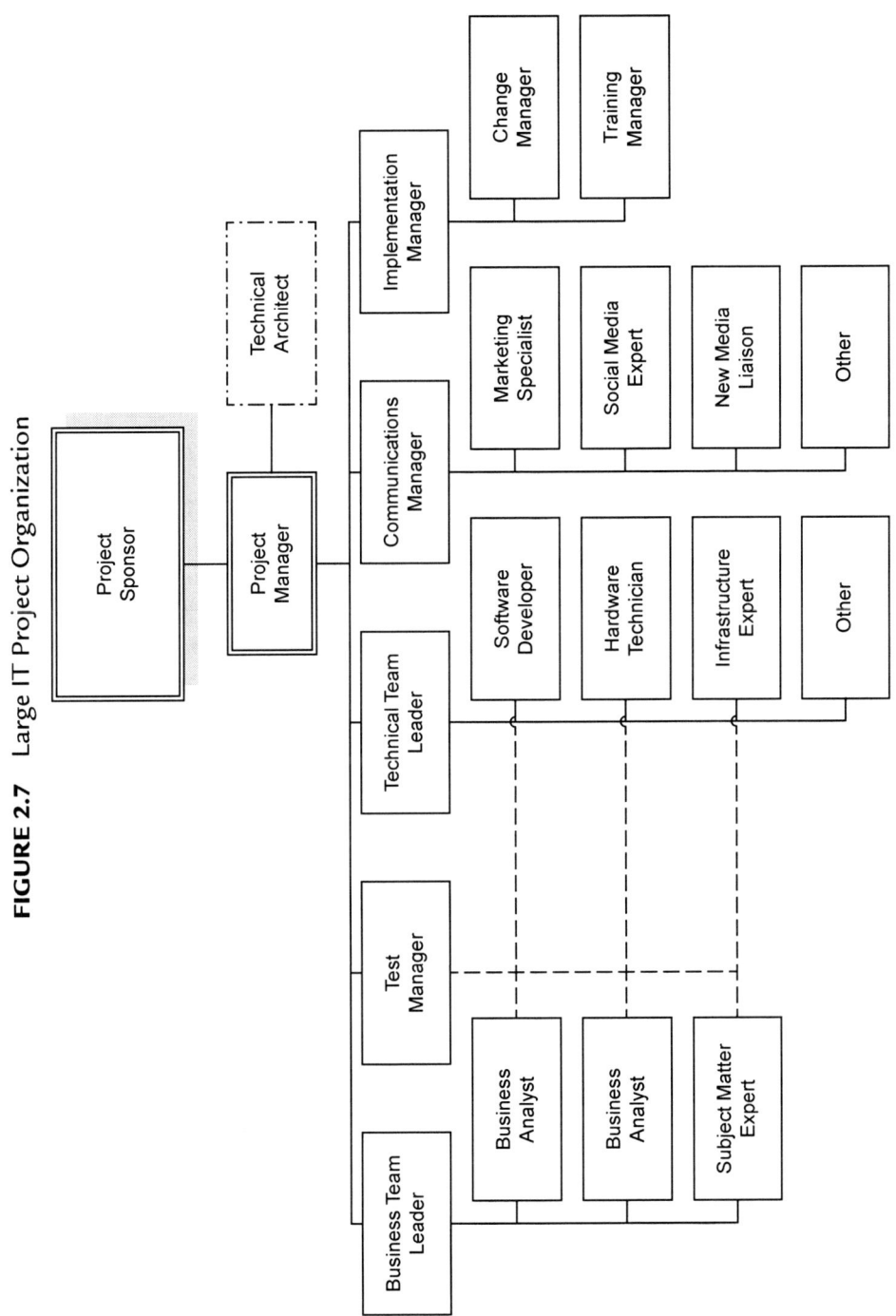

FIGURE 2.7 Large IT Project Organization

Q13 How do you organize for custom software development projects?

Consider a project where the goal is to custom-develop a new system, building it from scratch. In this instance, the team's crew of technical resources requires some depth. A system constructed from scratch—where the system is architected, the infrastructure is established, the software is written, and the database is constructed by the project team—requires a full suite of technical and business expertise. The technical team might be particularly heavy with software developers, database designers, and other highly qualified personnel.

Q14 How do you organize for COTS and transfer system projects?

The deployment and/or integration of a COTS or transfer system presents different challenges. A transfer system is similar to a COTS system in that the project plans to purchase a solution off the shelf from a vendor (COTS) or from a similar business or agency that has constructed its own system and made it available for purchase.

Depending on the size of the project, COTS system, and/or transfer system, the project team organizations remain generally the same (Figure 2.8). The software has already been crafted. The solution is being purchased out of the box or from another organization. On that basis, the need for software developers, database designers, and even the technical architect diminishes. Those skill sets might be called on when the project team encounters a unique challenge, but that would be very part-time.

Business team members remain in high demand for COTS and transfer system projects. Both types of systems require configuration to meet an organization's specific needs. Customization of COTS and transfer system products is common, and it must be supported by team members with a good understanding of the business need.

Q15 How do you organize for system modernization projects?

A system modernization project may require little by way of business expertise because the functional requirements for the system will not change substantially. If the project is effectively managed, system users will feel little, if any, impact. The project, perhaps more than any other type of IT project, becomes one of a technical nature, and the construction of the team reflects that emphasis (Figure 2.9).

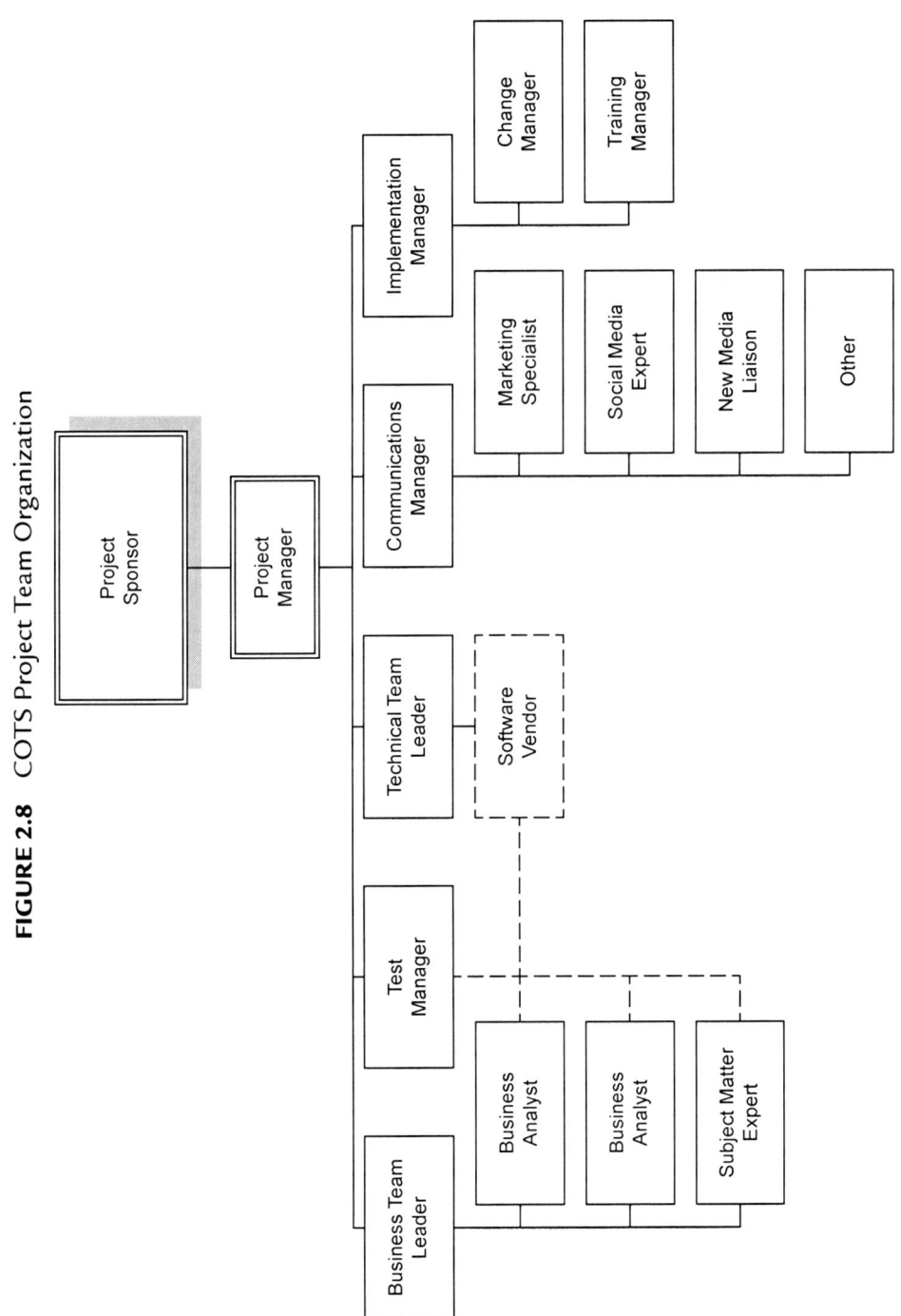

FIGURE 2.8 COTS Project Team Organization

FIGURE 2.9 System Modernization Project Organization

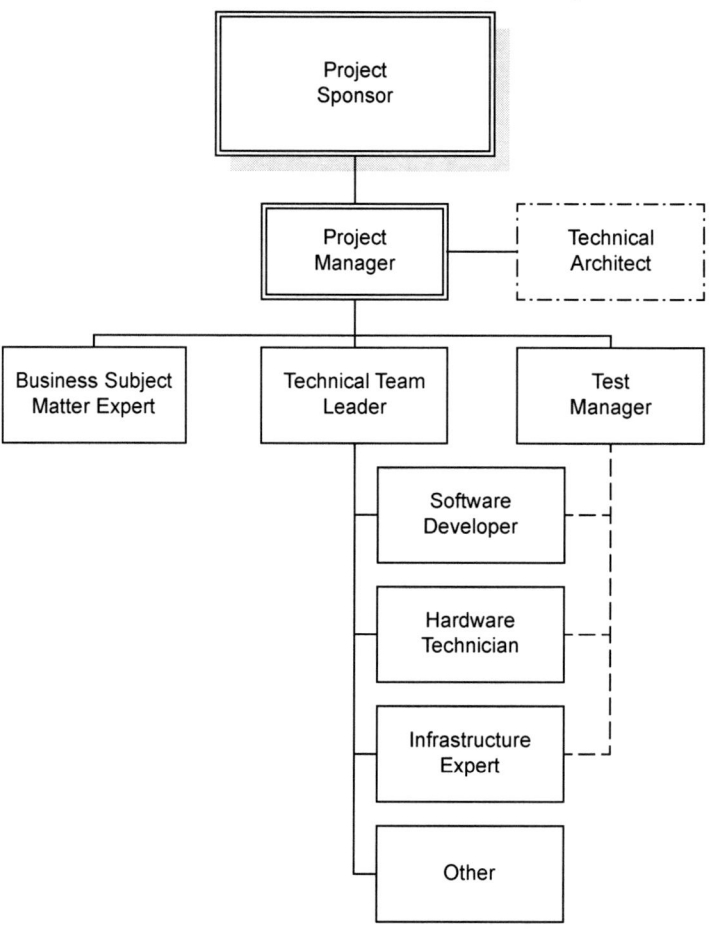

A software package integration project potentially involves a custom-developed or existing solution of which a software package is to be made a part. This type of project requires interfacing the software package with the custom software development solution. Essentially, doing so requires some additions to the team—the software package vendor and a crew of software integrators who are familiar with the software package. In this instance, the project structure is once again modified (Figure 2.10).

Q16 How do you organize for infrastructure upgrade projects?

Infrastructure upgrade projects perhaps lack some of the romance associated with developing new software applications, but they are nonetheless complex

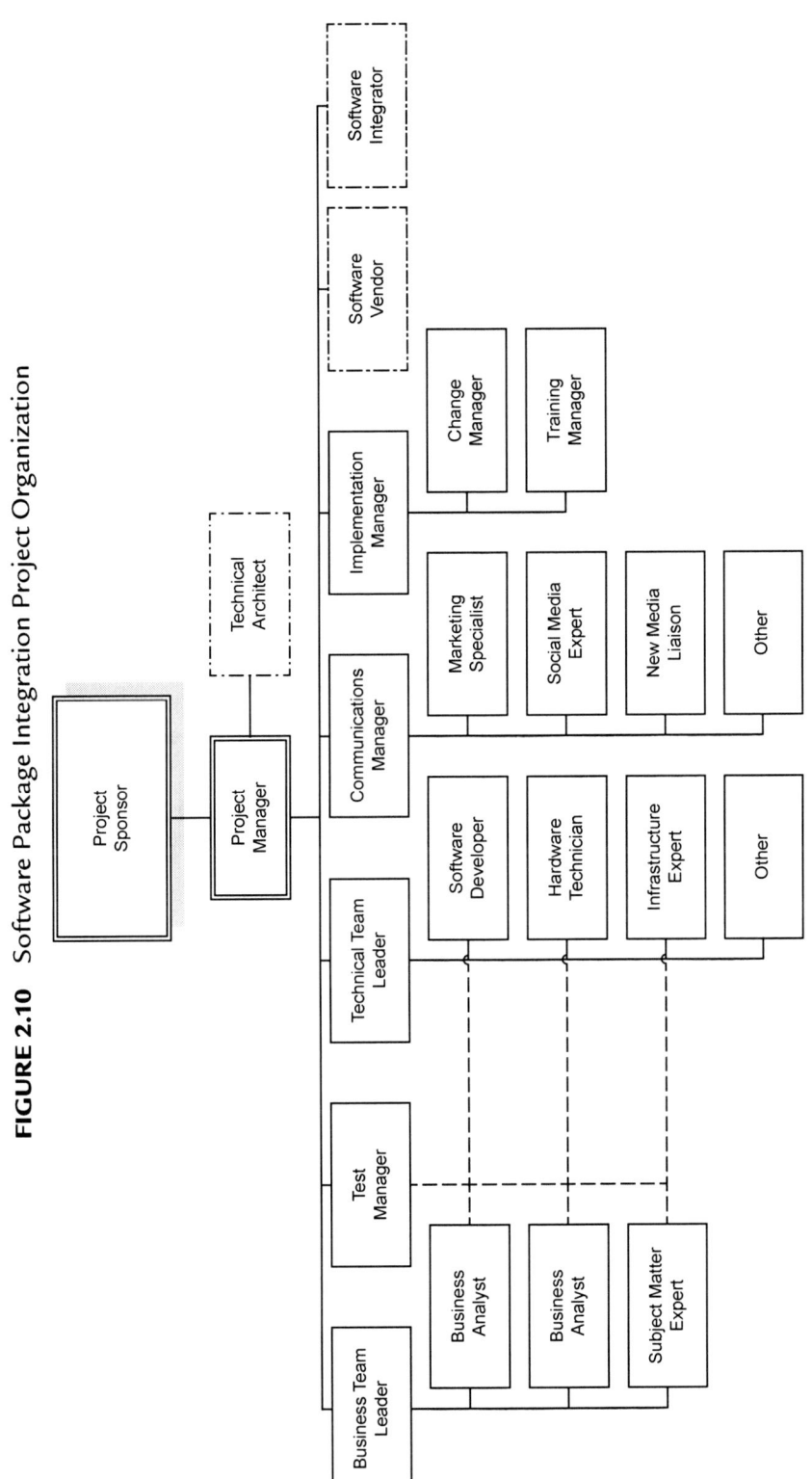

FIGURE 2.10 Software Package Integration Project Organization

undertakings that require a deliberate organizational approach. The team for a project like this can be pared down substantially because, if all goes well, the business community feels little impact. That said, careful project managers make sure all bases are covered by including the proper resources on the project team (Figure 2.11).

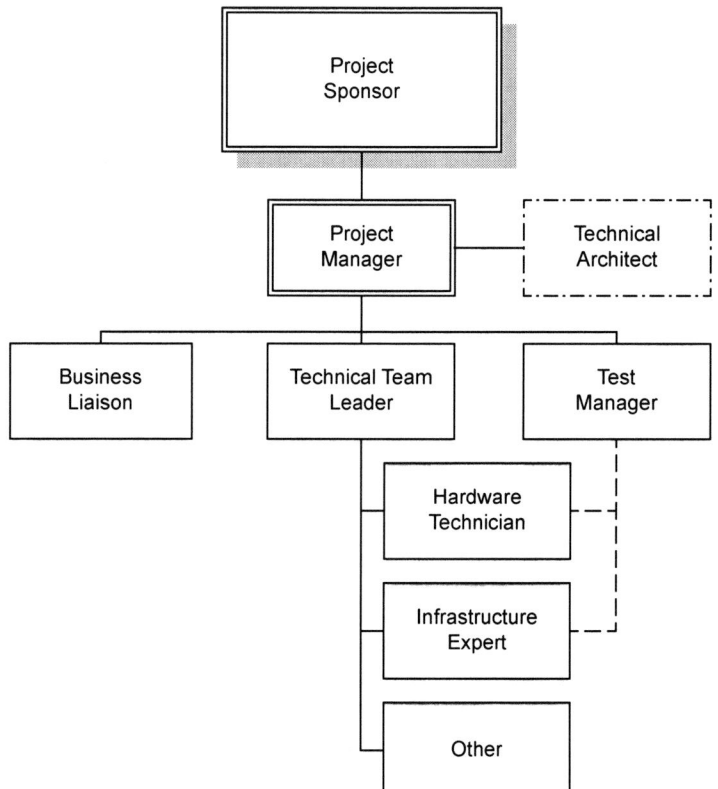

FIGURE 2.11 Infrastructure Upgrade Project Organization

Q17 Is the quality assurance analyst a member of the project team?

Quality assurance (QA) is a key skill set for any project team. The QA analyst stands apart from the team, reporting directly to the project sponsor. He observes from a distance as the project manager and her team develop and implement project plans and specifications. The QA analyst validates that processes are executed appropriately, identifies areas for improvement, and makes recommendations for implementing those improvements. The QA analyst reviews project artifacts and provides comments intended to increase the project's potential for success.

Too many times, QA analysts are perceived as grammar-checkers for project documents. That is a waste of time and money. A skilled QA analyst appreciates that it is not typos that affect a project's opportunity for success. Success comes from the ability to identify substantive, fundamental issues with project delivery and provide timely, practical recommendations for remediation.

PROJECT MANAGEMENT CONSIDERATIONS

Q1 What is the role of the IT project manager?

The IT project manager is the on-hand project team leader. That person's job is to plan and direct the day-to-day activities of the team, keep the project sponsor informed, and relate the project's vision and objectives to the project's team members and stakeholders.

Q2 Who makes the best project manager—a technologist or a businessperson?

In general, a good project manager with a solid general business background can do a credible job managing most IT projects. It is more difficult for a technical resource without that business background to serve as a project manager and successfully deliver a business-oriented IT project. As much as technical resources might understand the details of technical solution delivery, they often do not relate well with the nuances of business operations.

On the other hand, a major role of the IT project manager is to translate the business needs of the project into technical language that the project's technical resources can use to deliver an appropriate technical solution. The business-oriented IT project manager would do well, then, to gain some technical background if she wants to make a career in the field. It doesn't take much to start the process of technology familiarization. Any training in that area is likely to help the business-oriented project manager to better communicate with and relate to technical project team members.

The rarest and perhaps most effective form of IT project manager is the technologist who has successfully crossed over into the business domain at some point in his career. These persons are few and far between, but they offer a unique appreciation of both the business and technical sides of their projects and can be highly successful.

Q3 Who handles test management?

The project manager or a business analyst often takes on the role of test manager for a small IT project. For a larger project, there is often a separate test manager, who brings specific expertise to the project and develops the test plans, test scripts, and test cases that will be used to ensure the solution developed by the project team meets the organization's needs.

Frequently, the test manager has a test team that consists of users drawn from the organization, who test the system against the test plans. The project's business analysts might also function as part of the test team.

Q4 What is the role of the test manager?

The test manager might lead a substantial team of users, subject matter experts, technical resources, and business analysts at different points on the project. This person develops the project's test plans and must possess good writing skills. He should be adept at communicating system requirements in a manner that each of these types of team members can understand. The test manager coordinates, manages, and reports the progress of the test team and therefore must be well organized and a good communicator.

Q5 What is communications management?

For IT projects where external stakeholders are deeply involved, the risk is high, and there is much at stake, an additional key project team member is the communications manager. It is this person who plans and manages communications between the team and its stakeholders.

Where exposure to the public is low, project teams usually do not require that a separate person be assigned to this role. In such cases, the project manager often assumes the role of communications manager. For larger projects, however, deliberate communications planning and execution of communications plans are critical, and a communications expert might be brought onto the team for that specific purpose.

IT projects are notorious for coming in over budget, being late, and often failing outright. All too often, failures occur because expectations are not set appropriately and continuously updated with key stakeholders. A good communications manager can ensure that the expectations of stakeholders are managed appropriately, including modification of those expectations when project scope evolves and schedules extend beyond planned end dates.

Q6 What is the role of the communications manager?

Large, complex projects with many stakeholders might require a full- or part-time communications manager. This individual might supervise a diverse team of communications media staff, marketing resources, and public relations experts. It is the communications manager who crafts the project's communications plan and develops the communications matrix that is the backbone of that plan. She executes the project's communications plan and brings together the skill sets necessary to support the project manager's needs for the project.

Q7 What is a configuration manager?

If an IT project includes the need for software development, database modeling, hardware acquisition and configuration, and network design, a configuration manager is needed to pull all that together. It is the configuration manager who will document, store, record, and report the current version of the project's deliverables to the project team and ensure that everyone works from the same set of specifications.

The configuration manager advises the development team regarding which version of the database is most current, which version of the software is to be referenced by team members, and which hardware configuration is to support the technical solution.

Q8 What is the role of a technical architect?

The technical architect is often the most senior member of the technical team assigned to the project. A qualified technical architect typically has extensive background and experience in the areas of software, database, and network architecture. Although numerous certifications are available from software and hardware manufacturers, there are few consistent standards for what qualifies a person to be a technical architect, per se.

The role of technical architects is to set the stage for how a software and hardware solution will be implemented. They lay down the bones of the new system, network, and so on. Working with the technical team and potential system users, they define how the units of software will be organized, designed, and interfaced. They identify how any software packages will be integrated into the solution, if that requirement exists for the project. The technical architect may sketch out how the various pieces of the final deliverable solution will be meshed within the organization's infrastructure in the form of system and network diagrams. Figure 2.12 is an example of an n-tier architecture that might be provided by a technical architect.

FIGURE 2.12 Example of a Simple n-Tier Architecture Diagram

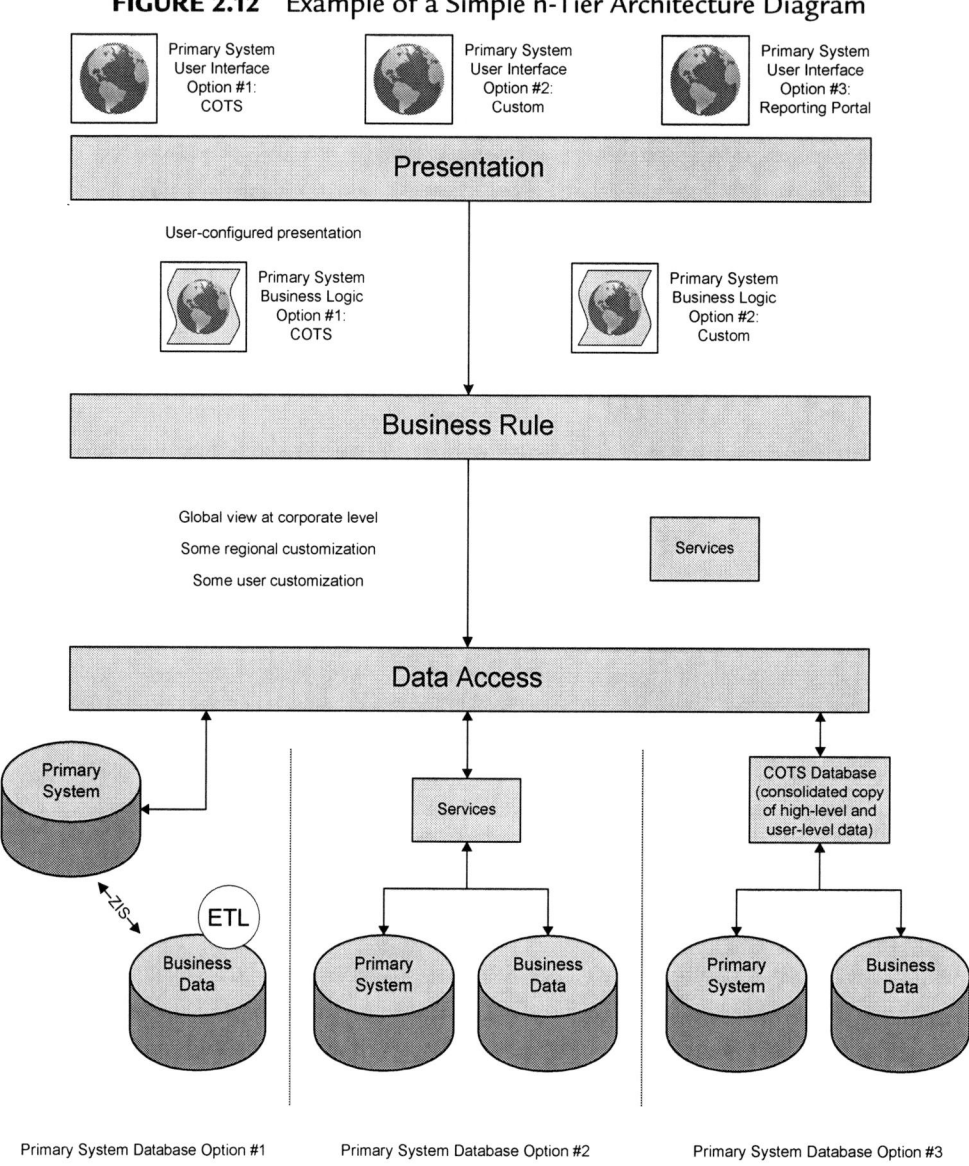

COTS = Commercial off the shelf; ETL = Extract, Transform, Load; ZIS = Zone integration software.

The technical architect develops the approach that the technical team will take to develop the project's solution. That can include identifying guidelines and standards that the technical team will use as the basis for their efforts. Once those standards and guidelines have been communicated to the technical team, the technical architect periodically reviews the team's progress and adherence to direction through code walk-throughs and reviews, and through discussions with the project team.

The technical architect is a source of information for the project team at large and a point of escalation for team members confronted by issues that cannot be resolved at the software developer, database modeler, or business analyst level.

The topics a technical architect commonly addresses include system security, interface types and approaches, development tools, infrastructure issues, communications issues within and external to the software and hardware solution, identification of technical risks and risk management strategies, and market research to identify alternative solutions for software development and hardware acquisition.

As in the project management field, anyone with any level of experience in software development and hardware integration can hang out a shingle and identify himself as a technical architect. To ensure that a candidate for the position is, in fact, qualified to do the job on your project, check the person's references and certifications and have another architect that you trust test the candidate to assess the validity of his claims.

Q9 What are SMEs, and what value do they provide to an IT project?

An SME is a subject matter expert. SMEs are people with a specific, detailed understanding of the business processes or technical tools that the IT project needs to deliver a quality technical solution.

SMEs come in many shapes and sizes. They may include the most senior person in the company or agency or the mail room delivery person. If an IT system is being constructed to support a business process, the person who understands that process is critical to the success of the IT project. An SME can be anyone who understands some aspect of the IT project that must be communicated to the technical team to support solution development.

The types of SMEs frequently seen on an IT project include:

- Business SMEs
  - Accounting
  - Human resource management
  - Operations management
  - Senior management
  - System users
  - Others
- Technical SMEs
  - Data security
  - Business infrastructure
  - Enterprise architecture standards and guidelines
  - Other

PROJECT INITIATION

Chapter 3

Successful projects do not just happen. They are conceived deliberately and planned in detail.

Organizations that invest in IT projects tend to enter into such efforts with cautious deliberation. They move forward in a stepwise manner, hedging their bets before going all in with their investment.

The deliberate process of deciding whether to invest in an IT project occurs during project initiation. It is during this phase that the project sponsor learns enough to determine whether to move a project forward with some confidence or set the project aside as ill-conceived.

PROJECT MANAGEMENT CONSIDERATIONS

Q1 What tasks are carried out during the project initiation process?

The goal of the project initiation phase is to develop an understanding of the basic elements of the project and describe the project in such a manner that the project sponsor can, with some confidence, authorize the project to move forward. The major deliverable provided during this phase of the project is the project charter.

A checklist of common tasks carried out during the initiation process of an IT project is provided as Figure 3.1.

FIGURE 3.1 IT Project Initiation Process Tasks

Task	Yes	No	NA
Is there a scope statement containing:			
1. Project justification (business need)			
2. Product description			
3. List of major deliverables			
4. Acceptance criteria—criteria for success			
5. Schedule constraints			
Is there a project charter?			
Have roles and responsibilities been defined?			
Is the client team clearly identified?			
Has a project manager been assigned?			
Has a technical lead/architect been assigned?			
Is there a budget?			
Hold a team kickoff meeting with the client?			
Hold an internal team kickoff meeting?			

Q2 What skill sets are needed for an IT project team during project initiation?

The team required to initiate a project and develop a project charter need not be large. By definition, a project charter should address high-level project plans, objectives, requirements, risks, costs, milestones, and so on. The project can be initiated by a relatively small staff of high-level project planners and technical resources. Those individuals, by role, include:

- *Project sponsor*—Approver of the project charter
- *Project manager*—Leads the initiation process and writes the project charter
- *Technical lead or architect*—Advisor/contributor to the project manager and project sponsor.

It is unlikely that the project sponsor will craft any significant portion of the project charter directly, but he must be present to ensure that his vision is clearly understood and appreciated by those who undertake that task.

Many organizations have strong feelings about whether the project manager should be assigned to a project before or after the project charter is completed. Sometimes a person is hired specifically for the job of developing the project charter. In rare cases, project charters are completed years before a project is finally authorized to proceed.

If a project manager is to be assigned to lead an IT project, she needs to know as much as possible about the project to ensure the project's success. That includes background about how decisions were made during the initiation process as well as other more subtle nuances about management perspectives when the project was initially discussed. All of this could reveal critical information that provides value later, as the project progresses through the planning, execution, and closure processes.

High-level technical expertise is required to ensure that the project charter addresses all possible technical considerations. Although it is true that IT projects are, in fact, business-oriented, business professionals who lack technical expertise might make assumptions about technology that are not reasonable. The addition of a senior technical resource to the project charter team can help avoid this situation and better frame the project's expectations.

The potential exists that this small band of professionals might require support from other areas of the business or technology industry. In those instances, subject matter experts can be called in to join the team for brief periods.

Q3 What is a vision statement?

No project team can expect to get anywhere without a good vision statement, published in writing and signed by the project sponsor. Once that document is signed by the project sponsor, the team can move forward with some confidence that the project's endpoint and criteria for success are clearly defined.

The typical vision statement for an IT project answers four very specific questions:

1. What benefit do the project sponsor and the organization expect to derive from the project?
2. Who will be impacted by the project?
3. How will things be different when the project has been completed?
4. What will the final product or solution look like when the project is complete?

It is all too common for IT projects to have no vision statement at all. From a project quality assurance perspective, that absence can spell the difference between success and failure. There's a saying in project management that summarizes this point: "If you can see it, you can get there. But if you can't see it, you are going nowhere."

With a clear vision statement in hand, the project team gains a sense of direction for the project. All matters of scope, schedule, and cost reflect back to that statement. If any effort that falls outside that vision is undertaken, it is out of scope. If a change request is submitted to modify the project's scope, the approved vision statement serves as a guide for determining whether that change request fits within the project sponsor's guidance to the team.

Q4 What role do project objectives play in an IT project?

Objectives are clear statements of the business value an organization expects to realize from a project. They spring directly from the project's approved vision statement, which addresses this issue at a high level. By definition, when the project's objectives have been satisfied, the project is done.

Objectives are expressed in SMART terms:

S—*Specific*. The benefit should address a singular aspect of business, or multiple aspects of business that can be addressed individually and wholly from an enterprise perspective.

M—*Measurable*. The benefit to the organization should be quantifiable. A goal of a percentage reduction in errors or increase in market share should be stated as a benchmark for project performance.

A—*Assignable*. Someone or some group within the organization should be willing to sign his name on a piece of paper stating that he needs a specific outcome and the functionality necessary to provide that specific, measurable benefit.

R—*Reasonable*. It is not true that if you throw enough money at an IT project, anything is possible. In some cases, the technology simply does not yet exist or the timeframe allowed for the project is unreasonable. If the money is not available in sufficient amounts, the goal ascribed to the project might be equally unreasonable.

T—*Time-bound*. A project should be achievable within a specific timeframe. If there is a need worth investing in, that need should be satisfied within a specific timeframe. If no urgency is associated with the need, it is doubtful that the organization will remain committed to the project for the time it takes to complete.

Any single project can have a number of objectives. An IT project with the goal of implementing a new human resource (HR) management information system might have the following objective, among others:

Decrease the number of payroll processing errors experienced by employees to zero by enabling employees to update and maintain personal and payment information in the HR system online, in near real-time.

This objective is sure to please employees if their employer has been plagued with issues related to inaccurate or outdated direct deposit banking data, or changes in employment status (e.g., promotions, changes of shift). If the objective is realized, the company can expect substantial improvement in employee morale.

The objective has numerous implications. The most obvious include the potential need for an online, Web-based employee data update capability. This suggests the need for a secure infrastructure that supports employee access to specific areas of the new system.

The objective also specifies near real-time access to employee data, once it has been updated, by payroll personnel. It suggests the need for active interfaces between those modules of the system that receive, store, and manage employee data and those responsible for calculating payroll information. The objective also suggests a need for those interfaces to move data through the system on a nearly constant basis, and to deposit funds into bank accounts outside the organization over the Internet.

A seasoned technical resource would consider the technological implications of the objective described above and quickly conclude that there are infrastructure, capacity, external interface, and security issues to be addressed for the project. This might result in an additional objective for the project with a technical rather than business focus.

Technical objectives are often referred to as implied objectives because they are implied or suggested by the requirements identified within the construct of a business objective. In this case, the implied objective might be stated as follows and included in the IT project's charter and other planning documents:

Upgrade existing infrastructure to enable the new HR management information system to receive input online and transmit funds through external interfaces, while supporting existing security guidelines and standards as well as bandwidth and data storage sufficient to support personnel data needs.

IT project business objectives always have technological implications. Acquiring the services of a senior, experienced technical resource can help you identify those implications and address them within your project.

DELIVERABLES

Q1 What is a deliverable?

Deliverables are the things produced and delivered during the course of a project. The end product or IT system provided by the project is a deliverable. Other deliverables might include the things that are produced that lead up to the delivery and implementation of the final deliverable system, such as hardware, software, firmware, design documents, project planning documents, and reports.

Project deliverables should be reviewed and approved in every instance. If a deliverable is technical in nature, the project's technical lead or architect can provide the best perspective for reviewing that deliverable. If the deliverable is a business requirements specification, the project's business team leader might be the best person to review that product. The approval authority for any deliverable produced for a project is the project manager or project sponsor, even though he might delegate that responsibility to another team member.

When a deliverable is approved, the approval should be documented. Formal, written approval, however briefly stated, provides evidence that the resources expended to provide that deliverable were not spent in vain. This becomes particularly important if a project is to be audited or subject to external quality assurance checks over the course of the effort.

Q2 What is a business case and why is it important?

The business case is an elaboration on the benefit portion of the vision statement. A business case provides the rationale for investing in an IT project. It addresses how much that investment might be, the benefits the organization will net once the project is completed, and the risks associated with the undertaking. How that business case is expressed varies from organization to organization. Some require a narrative, subjective assessment of these points; others require a more objective analysis with charts, tables, and pro forma cost and revenue projections.

For very small projects, the business case might be derived over coffee and annotated on a handy napkin or piece of scratch paper. For larger projects, where more money is at risk, the business case might take the form of an extensive, formally delivered report. No matter the format, the business case should, in every instance, spell out why the project is a good thing to do for the organization.

Metrics are an important part of a business case. Although the business case might focus on a perceived need for change that an IT solution could provide, the drivers of that change, the costs associated with the effort to realize that change, and the expected return constitute the content of the business case.

Figure 3.2 shows how a formal business case might be organized for a business considering whether to undertake an IT project.

FIGURE 3.2 Business Case Template

I. Project Definition
1. Business Objectives: The project's purpose; expected end results
2. Focus: Organization-centric areas of emphasis
Owning Office: External: Internal: Political:
3. Context: Other factors that might affect project success
Assumptions:
Constraints:
Definitions:
Issues:
Risks:
Other:
4. Partners: Other organizations participating in this project

II. Proposed Solution	
1. General Description of Proposed Solution	
2. Benefits: How the solution will improve the business	
Measurable Service:	
Reduced Cost:	
3. Feasibility: Positive or negative factors that could affect the project's success, from project start until the solution is in place	

(continues)

(continued)

II. Proposed Solution					
Explanation:					
Risk:	1 [ ]	2 [ ]	3 [ ]	4 [ ]	5 [ ]
	High Risk				Low Risk
4. Sustainability: Factors that could affect the project's success once the solution is deployed, over the product's lifecycle					
Explanation:					
5. Anticipated Project Risks Risk #1: Risk #2 Etc.					
Overall Risk Rating:	1 [ ]	2 [ ]	3 [ ]	4 [ ]	5 [ ]
	High Risk				Low Risk
6. Estimated Project Cost					
Project Costs: Life Cycle Costs:					
5. Alternate Solutions Considered, with Assessment					

Q3 What is a feasibility study and why is it important during project initiation?

A feasibility study defines whether an IT project can be completed in a reasonable timeframe, at a reasonable cost, with the technology and skills that are available today. If there are multiple options for satisfying an IT need, the feasibility study identifies those options. The report spells out the risks, benefits, costs, and organizational issues for each alternative and recommends the best approach for the organization. A feasibility study should be completed before the project charter is developed and approved by the project sponsor.

In conducting a feasibility study, it is important to avoid bias. All too often, organizations determine a need for an IT solution based on a vendor's savvy marketing presentation or an executive's excitement over a new technology viewed in passing at an industry conference. Although the organization's need might be real, there are likely many technologies and vendors that could deliver a sound technical solution to support that need—all with varying costs, risks, benefits, and complexities. The goal of a feasibility study is to determine which of those solutions are likely to provide the best value for the investment in an impartial, unbiased manner.

Once the feasibility study has been completed, a report presenting the findings is prepared. Common elements of an IT project feasibility study report include:

- Executive summary
- Summary of the business case
- Objectives (the business value provided by the project)
- Impacts on other organizations, people, and within the sponsoring organization
- Change management issues (how the organization will change as a result of the solution provided by the project)
- Major alternatives considered
- Proposed solution
- Strategic fit—how the proposed solution supports the organization's business strategy
- Project management approach and resource requirements projected for completing the project
- Estimated duration of the project and a high-level work plan
- Cost–benefit analysis to compare both project and lifecycle costs and benefits

THE PROJECT CHARTER

Q1 What is a project charter?

The project charter is a decision document signed by the project sponsor. It is authored by the project manager and describes the project in sufficient detail for the project sponsor to determine whether proceeding with the project is a good idea. A signed project charter authorizes a project to move forward and delegates authority to the project manager. Once signed, the project charter concludes the initiation process for a project.

Q2 What is included in an IT project charter?

The project charter for an IT project differs little in terms of format and content from a charter developed for a non-IT project. If there are any differences, they appear in the form of a business case that specifically calls out the need for an IT solution.

A project charter should be tailored to meet the needs of a specific project and should be organized in a manner that supports the organization's culture. If the organization is risk averse, more space in the document should be dedicated to risk management, and requirements should be defined at a more detailed level. If the organization is more accepting of risk, less space need be invested in defining detailed requirements. That effort and expense can be deferred until the planning phase, after the project sponsor has determined whether the project should proceed.

Project charters should contain the minimum information necessary for the project sponsor to develop a good sense of the project and approve it to move forward. The document should be as brief as possible. Too much information and the document and project sponsors are not likely to read it. They are busy people and, as the signature authority for any project, deserve the benefit of brevity. As a rule, keep project charters short and to the point.

Common elements addressed in most IT project charters are outlined in Figure 3.3.

FIGURE 3.3 Project Charter Development Checklist

Description	Yes	No	NA
Vision statement			
Business problem, need or opportunity			
Project objectives			
Description of the product to be produced			
High level schedule/milestones			
Project governance			
Roles and responsibilities			
Assumptions and constraints			

Major deliverables			
High-level risks			
Initial stakeholder analysis			
Budget and budget management			
Project charter approval form			
Appendix—High-level scope statement			
Appendix—High-level requirements			

Q3 What deliverables are identified in the project charter?

Figure 3.4 provides a list of deliverables commonly identified in IT project charters:

FIGURE 3.4 Deliverables Listed in IT Project Charters

Project Charter Sample Deliverables List
• Business case (if not previously completed)
• Feasibility study (if not previously completed)
• Investment plan (if not previously completed)
• Preliminary scope statement
• Budget management plan
• Change control plan
• Communications plan
• Integrated project management plan
• Issue management plan
• Risk management plan
• Stakeholder management plan
• System requirements specification
• Test management plan
• Training management plan
• Others

Q4 Do you need detailed requirements before you can publish a project charter?

The project charter is a decision document that enables the project sponsor to determine whether the project can be reasonably expected to provide the prescribed scope within budget and schedule constraints. From that standpoint, whether detailed requirements are a necessary component of the project charter depends on each specific project's situation.

High-level requirements are reasonably simple to generate. They evolve directly from the project's business objectives. A small team of business analysts, with the help of a few subject matter experts, can generate a good set of high-level business requirements in a reasonably short time. Given that list of high-level business requirements, it is reasonably simple for an experienced technical resource to develop a complementary set of high-level technical requirements.

Organizations with a poor track record of IT project success might become risk averse because of those bad experiences. It is common for this sort of organization to require a detailed understanding of a project's requirements before approving a project to move forward. In such a case, detailed requirements become an essential element of a project charter's table of contents.

Constructing a comprehensive set of detailed business and technical requirements for an IT project can be an expensive, time-consuming effort. Input from the project's user group is required to break down the high-level requirements to the point where the project team can estimate the work needed to satisfy them. The same is required of the technical team, which must approach the project's technical requirements with equal attention to detail.

It is not uncommon for efforts to document a project's detailed requirements to continue for months and involve dozens of resources. If detailed requirements must be included in a project charter, the sponsoring organization must be prepared to absorb the associated cost.

If a project contains little risk, if similar projects have been completed regularly by the same organization, or if project objectives specify functionality that is common and well known within an industry, the organization might feel little need to include detailed requirements in the project charter.

Chapter 4

PROJECT PLANNING

When the project sponsor signs off on a project charter, her signature signifies the decision to move forward with the next step of the project—project planning. This approval suggests a willingness to invest the time and resources necessary to plan the project in detail, bring on a project team, and position the team to execute the project's detailed plans.

A project without a good plan is like a ship adrift in a foggy sea: There is little sense of direction. The opportunity for getting off course greatly increases. Good planning saves time and money, and it significantly increases a project's chances for success.

PROJECT MANAGEMENT CONSIDERATIONS

Q1 When does the project planning process begin for an IT project?

If the world was a neat, tidy, organized place, project planning would begin immediately following the conclusion of the project initiation process. The project sponsor would sign off on the project charter, and the planning process would begin. The project would progress in a neat, linear manner that everyone could depend on (Figure 4.1).

FIGURE 4.1 Linear Project Management Life Cycle

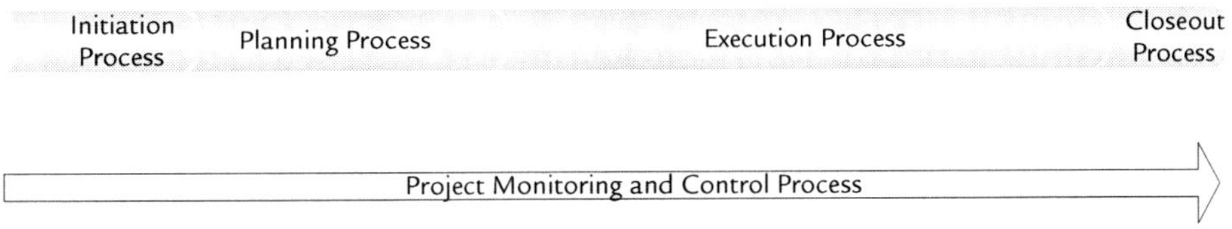

Initiation Process → Planning Process → Execution Process → Closeout Process

Project Monitoring and Control Process

IT projects sometimes work out that way. More often than not, they don't. They become messy affairs, with the initiation, planning, and execution processes overlapping (Figure 4.2). This occurs for many reasons, most of which are more practical than predictable.

FIGURE 4.2 Realistic Project Life Cycle Model

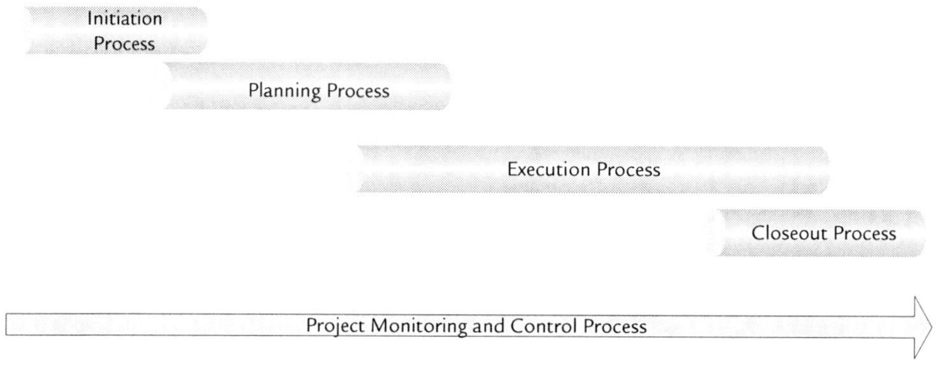

- Initiation Process
- Planning Process
- Execution Process
- Closeout Process
- Project Monitoring and Control Process

Consider an IT project team seeking authorization to proceed with an effort to fulfill a valid business need for an organization. The project sponsor directs the project manager to develop a project charter as part of the initiation process, before any detailed planning takes place. As the team develops the charter, they come across information that might be useful later, during detailed planning, but is not pertinent to the effort to complete the project's charter. If IT projects were perfectly linear affairs, they would cast that information aside until project initiation was complete and the project charter approved.

No project management professional in her right mind casts aside valuable information when it becomes available, simply because she is currently focused on the project charter. The professional analyzes the information, catalogs it, and stores it for use later at a more appropriate time. Because of the team's unintended acquisition and storage of detailed planning data, they have entered the planning process of the project, however inadvertently.

Consider the organization with a terrible track record of failed IT projects. As a result of their past experience with IT projects, that organization's management team might require additional, more detailed information before moving ahead with a project. In that case, they demand that detailed requirements be included in the initiation process. Project teams commonly produce detailed requirements as part of the project planning process. In the example of the risk-averse organization, generating those detailed requirements during the initiation process effectively started detailed planning in parallel with project initiation.

The answer to the question of when the planning process begins for an IT project is that it depends on the situation. The project initiation and planning phases overlap to some extent for every project. For ease of reference, most project managers default to the point in time when the project charter is signed when referring to the end of the project initiation process and the beginning of the project planning process.

Q2 Who designs a new IT system—the technical team, the business team, or the users?

The purpose of an IT solution is to provide business value to the organization. From that standpoint, the business team is best positioned to develop a new system's functional design. They work with the users to define project requirements and with the technical team to translate those requirements into something that can be constructed.

Business teams seldom possess all the skills necessary to create architecture for a technical solution or develop software that will serve the organization's business needs. The business team usually teams up with the technical team to combine their collective skills. When this happens, the question of who's in charge often comes up.

The business people want a solution that meets their needs and are most likely paying for that opportunity. The technical staff realizes that once a solution is constructed, they will be required to maintain and support it. Each has a stake in the outcome of the project and has needs they feel must be met. In some organizations, the situation degrades to a level of frustration and turf jealousy that impedes the project's progress.

Both groups have some ownership of the project and the design processes that lead to a satisfactory technical solution. Both perspectives contribute to the creation of a satisfactory design for that solution. The project manager's charge is to foster an atmosphere of collaboration between the two teams if the project is to realize the best possible outcome for the organization.

Q3 Is project planning different for different types of IT projects?

The planning requirements for an IT project vary depending on whether the specifications call for a software package implementation, a custom-built solution, or an integrated solution that leverages both approaches. Infrastructure enhancements carry their own set of needs, which differ from the others. Those variations in project type generally talk to the level of detail contained in a project plan, rather than the higher-level, over-arching processes included in the plan.

Transfer system projects mimic software package deployments. The goal of a transfer system project is to implement a system that has been used elsewhere by another similar organization. The risks associated with such a project, as well as the work plan, are generally the same as those for software package implementation.

Traditional project management methodologies dictate a basic framework that applies regardless of the type of solution desired by the user. The most common of these is referred to as a waterfall approach. The term *waterfall* comes from the fact that the project flows in a linear fashion from project initiation through project closeout. The basic elements of a waterfall approach that can be used for an IT project are depicted in Figure 4.3.

The specific sub tasks within a waterfall project plan vary for software package, custom-built, and integrated solutions. For example, there are likely to be more software development activities, code reviews, unit tests, and so on in custom software development projects. Software package implementations rely on pre-developed software. Unless substantial customization of the software package is required, code development activity can be kept to a minimum. Beyond that, the major elements of the different types of IT projects generally remain consistent.

Q4 What is Agile project delivery?

A relatively new approach to software development involves the Agile project delivery methodology. Agile is a software-centric instance of Lean Management. Agile empowers the project team to plan, develop, test, and demonstrate in rapid fashion. Project planning is much abbreviated and lasts as little as three days before software development actually begins. There is no project manager, schedule, or written project plan per se. Agile is quite a departure from traditional project delivery methodologies, but it is well suited for complex projects in organizations that are comfortable about empowering teams of individuals to work with relative autonomy.

In Agile, the process starts with the development of a capability map, rather than a traditional list of requirements. Stories are created that describe the perspective of each potential user, the capability the user needs the system to provide, and why the user needs it. Figure 4.4 shows a typical capability map containing several actual stories developed for a recent IT project.

Chapter 4 • Project Planning 59

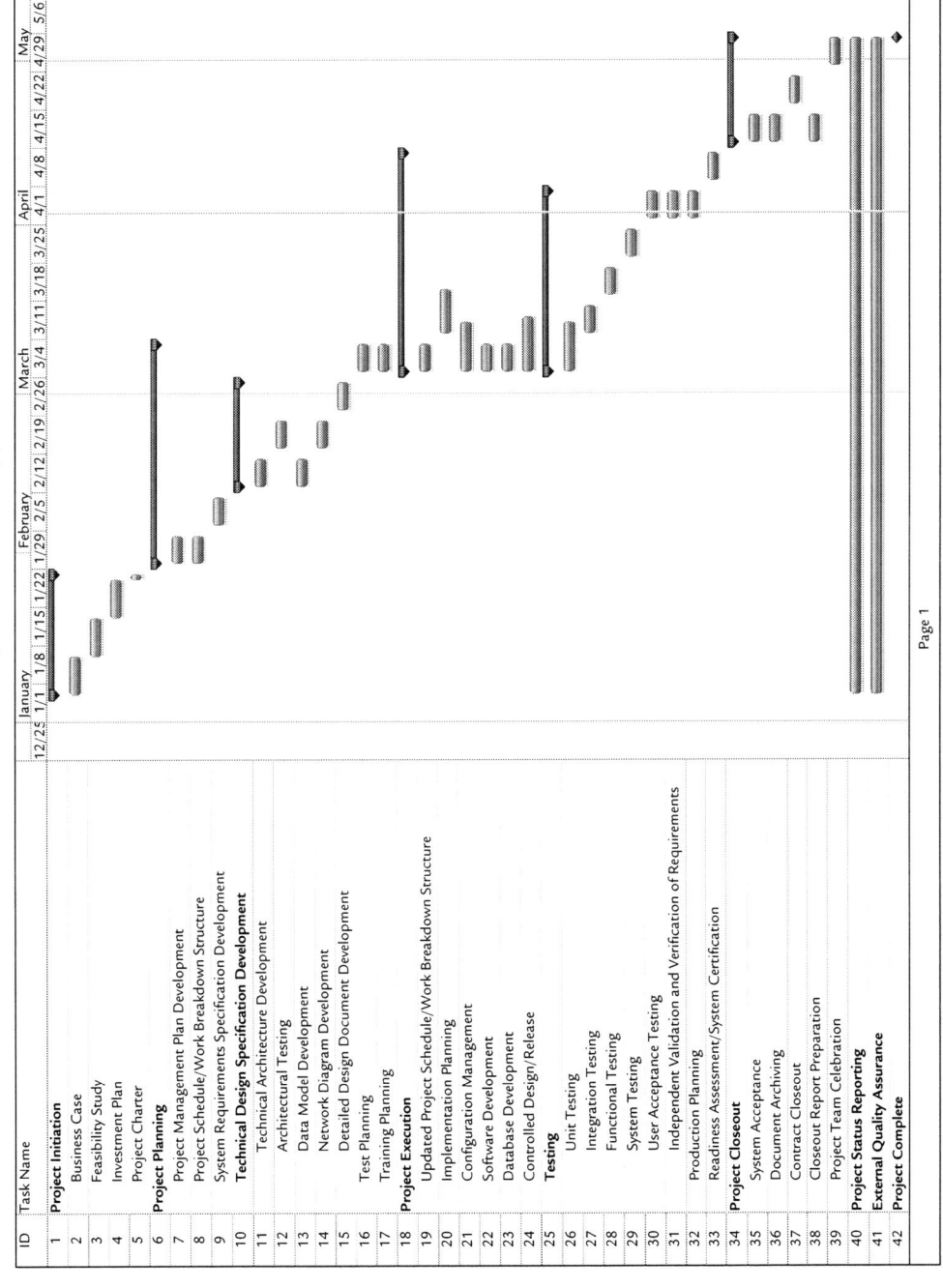

FIGURE 4.3 IT Project Waterfall Approach

FIGURE 4.4 Agile Process Capability Map

Priority H/M/L	Story #	Perspective	Story
H	T 1	Teacher/ Counselor/PLC	<u>Need</u>: I need to see and print out my students' achievement, behavioral, and evidence-based risk data in a simple, easy-to-view format that identifies trends at the summary level for classes and students, with data drill down capability using IT-neutral navigation <u>Value</u>: So that I can successfully identify performance trends at the classroom, student, and intervention group levels, for potential intervention and collaboration with peers.
H	T 6	Teacher/PLC	<u>Need</u>: I need access to current curriculum that supports the unique needs of my students and is validated against a solid body of evidence <u>Value</u>: So that I can improve student performance when curriculum currently in place no longer supports desired student outcomes.
H	P 1	Principal/ Counselor/ RTI-DEWIS Coordinator/ Coach	<u>Need</u>: I need access to all information provided to the teachers in my building/school as well as a summary view and reports of my school's/building's student achievement, behavior, and graduation risk data <u>Value</u>: So that I can regularly review the progress of students, classrooms, grades, and the school/building against core standards and other key performance indicators.
H	SD 1	School District Superintendent/ District Team	<u>Need</u>: We need all the capabilities identified for the Principals plus summary data and trending for the district as a whole <u>Value</u>: So that we can monitor student progress and identify opportunities for improvement.
H	SD 4	School District Superintendent/ District Team	<u>Need</u>: We need to be able to analyze and compare building- and district-level trend data regarding: • outcomes with specific curricula/interventions (including outcomes with specific populations), • cost (actual materials/license as well as training/ support to implement), and • ability to achieve fidelity <u>Value</u>: So that we can determine the most effective use of resources.

The project manager takes on the role of program manager, facilitates the team's needs, and reports to management regarding team process. Agile projects are time blocked and have a definite target completion date; however, a schedule is not developed in the traditional sense.

Each step of the process is time bound, and the overall availability of time for the project to deliver a final product is equally constrained (Figure 4.5). Note that the project team begins constructing some aspect of the system within four days of project initiation.

FIGURE 4.5 Agile Process Summary

Step #	Phase Title	Duration	Activity
1	Discovery	3 days	• A capability map is the deliverable • The capability map is prioritized by management in order of value to the organization
2	Rolling wave planning	6 hours	• Plan (estimate) to do one iteration • Plan two additional iterations into the future • Repeat as needed
3	Iteration planning	2 hours	• The team pulls capabilities from the capability map, now referred to as the *project backlog* • Team organizes to complete the work necessary to fill those requirements
4	Iteration	8 days	• Do the work • Involve the users • Test constantly
5	Review or demonstration	4 hours	• Demonstration of something real • Anything that's not done is considered waste and returned to the backlog • The goal is to demonstrate tangible products with functional value
6	Retrospective	4 hours	• Gather and discuss lessons learned from the last cycle
7	Repeat	Not applicable	Repeat steps 3 through 6, pulling more work from the backlog until the cost of additional work exceeds the value delivered to the user.

If an organization is accustomed to operating with a project schedule, its need can be accommodated, although what it will receive will be quite different from the norm. An example of an Agile approach to addressing a complex custom software development project is provided in Figure 4.6.

Agile projects do have budgets, but each task that the Agile team tackles does not have a specific cost assigned to it in advance.

Agencies and businesses that have low levels of project management maturity or that value highly controlled business environments do not usually embrace Agile. On the other hand, evidence over past years suggests that organizations that can adapt to a team-centric approach and adopt an Agile methodology typically deliver projects faster and at lower cost.

There seems to be a rule with IT projects: They are always more complex than they seem to be. From that standpoint, an Agile approach to planning and executing IT projects is recommended if the organization is prepared to adopt the team-centric approach upon which Agile is based.

Q5 How do you include users in the planning phase of an IT project?

One of the axioms of project management is to involve the users early and often during the course of an IT project.

IT projects exist to provide business users and their organizations with some sort of value that benefits their businesses. When it comes right down to it, the only people who matter are the users when the question involves planning how best to construct a new system or modify an organization's infrastructure. From that perspective, it is better to engage the users early in the project, when requirements are being identified, right through to production release of the technical solution. The users are the subject matter experts for the project, they constitute the most effective testers, and they provide critical insight into the project solution's needs.

The acid test for identifying the right user to enlist as an subject matter expert for a project is the closeness of that person's role to the organization's core business functions. Identify the key business processes of the organization, identify the people who carry out those processes, and you have identified the people who should be included in the project's detailed planning process. Those people are the users who can provide what the team needs to plan the project as efficiently and effectively as possible.

Q6 What is business architecture?

Business architecture is a business analysis and design approach that identifies an organization's functional business processes and documents the min the form of diagrams and other documentation. Using the business architecture approach, an

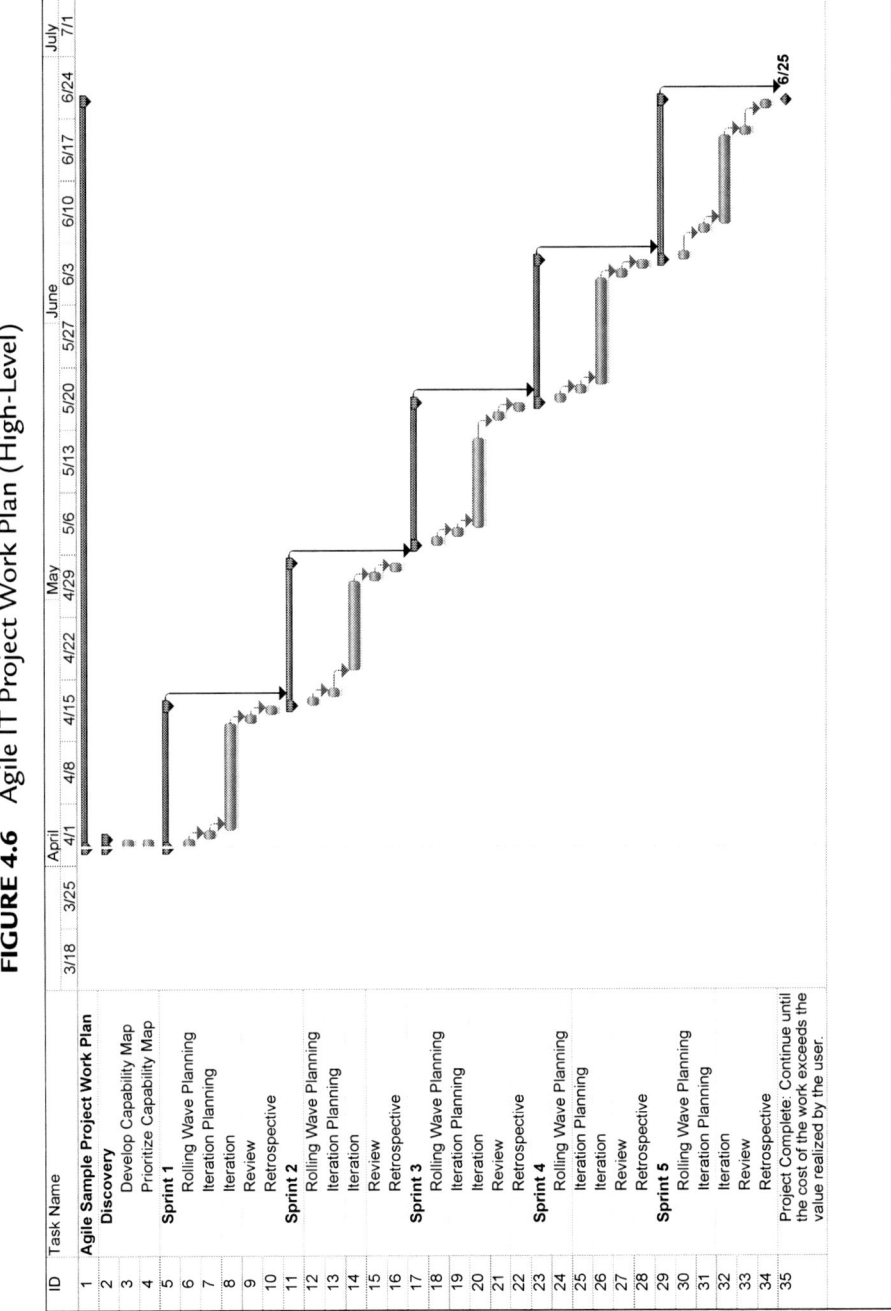

FIGURE 4.6 Agile IT Project Work Plan (High-Level)

organization's strategic goals are aligned with high-level business processes. The high-level business processes are decomposed to increasing levels of granularity to the extent necessary to align system functionality necessary to support those processes.

Figure 4.7 depicts the simple business architecture for a company's new marketing department. An IT project conceived to support this organization would use the diagram as a starting point to create a vision of the major business processes that must be modeled and supported by a new IT system. In this instance, these elements are depicted as the lower level of business processes that support the marketing strategy—market analysis, research and development, and so on.

FIGURE 4.7 High-Level Business Architecture

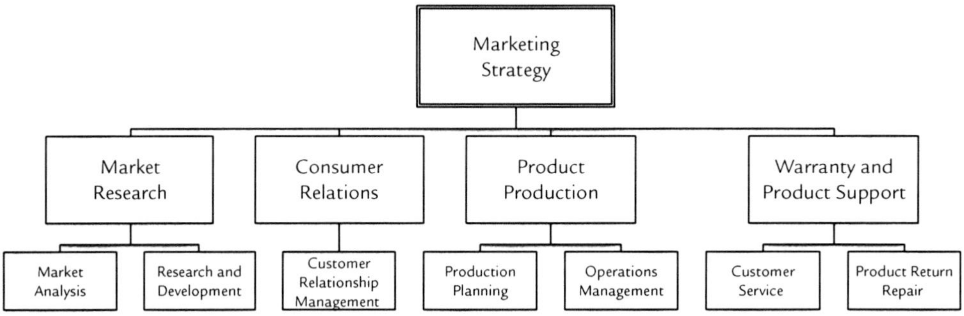

Once completed, the business architecture bridges the divide between the business processes that an organization needs and the subsystems of a potential new system that must be constructed to support the organization's business strategy (Figure 4.8).

FIGURE 4.8 Business Architecture Trace to System Requirements

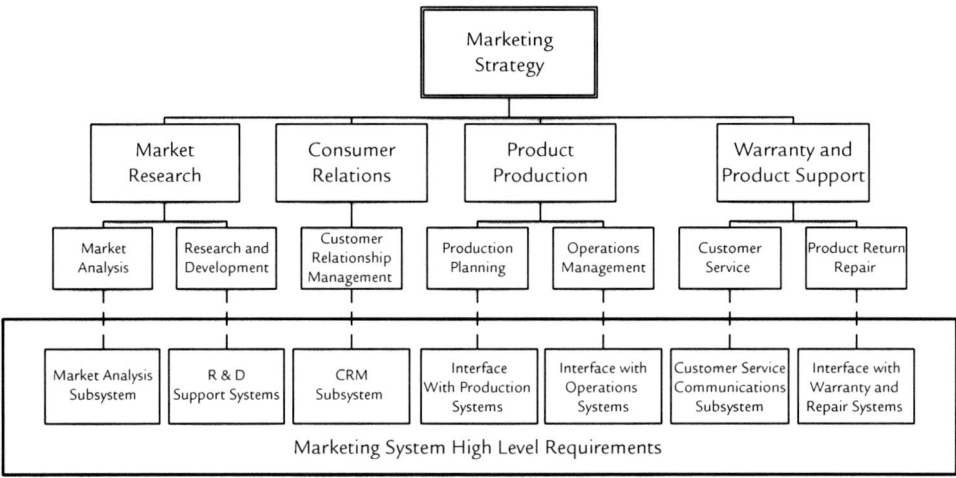

Q7 What is a network architecture and what role does it play in IT project planning?

A network architecture documents the conceptual framework into which a new system or its subsystems are built. A network diagram is a graphic representation of the elements of a system or series of systems, which depicts the nodes and connections amongst nodes within that system. Graphic symbols can be used to show common elements of the network, such as internal and external devices that communicate within that network.

The idea that standard icons and graphic representations are used in network diagrams and documents depicting network architecture is a myth. Technical architects frequently make up new terms and graphics as they develop their deliverables. Care should be taken to define the terms and symbols in any network architecture document generated for a project. Network diagrams describe the system and its relationship to other systems and elements of an organization's infrastructure at a very high level.

Q8 What is data migration and how do you plan for it?

Data migration includes planning and executing the movement of data from a source system to another destination system.

In IT projects, data migration often involves moving data that was configured for access by a legacy system to a new system based on completely different technology. That migration of data can create significant challenges in that the new system might reject the migrated data because of differences in how the data is configured.

In IT project management, the rule of thumb is that data migration is always difficult, no matter how simple it might seem at the onset. It always takes more time than anticipated and costs more than estimated.

The steps of the data migration process include identifying and defining the data to be migrated, mapping that data from the source system to the new destination, and testing the data to ensure it was migrated successfully. Often the project team discovers that the data must be converted to a new format, moving away from the data conventions of the old system or storage technology, to accommodate the new system's software platform.

Manual mapping, conversion, and migration of data can be extremely cumbersome and provide many opportunities for error. Some automated tools to assist with the data migration process are available on the market, and they should be considered for large projects with substantial amounts of data to move from one system to another, and with great differences between the legacy system's technology and that of the replacement system.

With complex system replacement projects, data migration is managed as a project of its own. It is analyzed, planned, executed, and tested prior to the actual migration. Figure 4.9 is a data migration plan checklist that has been used successfully in the past.

FIGURE 4.9 Data Migration Plan Checklist

Data Migration Plan Content	Yes	No	NA
Goal of the data migration effort			
Description of the project			
Major milestones			
Deliverables			
Objectives			
Data migration approach			
Success criteria			
Assumptions and constraints			
Resource requirements			
Roles and responsibilities			
Management and control			
Document signature and authorizations			

Q9 How do you relate project status to a nontechnical project sponsor?

Keep the report simple and to the point. Technical background is not a prerequisite for becoming a project sponsor. It is the responsibility of the project manager to translate any technical language that might appear in a project status report into terms that can be read, understood, and appreciated by the project's sponsor. By definition, the project sponsor is paying for the project; he deserves that sort of consideration.

Data provided in a project status report should not be overly technical. The goal of the project status report is to provide an objective assessment of the project's condition and position with regard to scope, schedule, and cost. These are not technical terms; they are concepts any business person can understand.

Project status reports typically include a *dashboard*, or visual representation of a project's status that includes red (unsatisfactory), yellow (cautionary), and green (satisfactory) indicators for areas such as scope, schedule, and cost. Project status reports include, as a minimum, a summary of the project's overall health, a list of tasks completed during the reporting period, tasks scheduled to be completed during the next reporting period, and a list of issues that require immediate attention from the project sponsor or stakeholders. More complex projects address each of these items as well as providing a summary of scope management activity on the project and key risks active at the time of the report. They may also include the results of an earned value analysis, which describes the project's performance to schedule and cost, along with any variances that have been identified and estimates to complete.

Figure 4.10 provides an example of a simple project status report. When writing any project status report, remember that project sponsors and stakeholders are busy business professionals. Keep the report as brief as possible. As a rule, one- and two-page reports can and will be read by a project sponsor. Longer reports tend to be skimmed with much of the content lost during the reading.

Q10 What is requirements traceability and why is it important for IT projects?

Requirements traceability offers a highly effective approach for ensuring that the requirements identified by the user are designed, built into, and tested for a new IT system. Traceability is not an esoteric approach to IT management; it is a "dirty elbows" methodology for guaranteeing that an IT system is built as the users intended.

Requirements are what a project team builds or acquires to fulfill the objectives of an IT project. Objectives are statements of the value an IT system is to provide a business. Objectives are derived directly from the approved vision statement, signed by the project's sponsor. These three relationships form the basis of requirements traceability.

If every requirement identified in a project's specification can be traced to an approved project objective, the project team and sponsor can rest assured that all of the system's desired functionality has been addressed. Requirements that cannot be traced to one or more project objectives are extraneous and out of scope.

On the other hand, during the course of designing or testing a new system, a project team member might identify a new requirement that cannot be related to an approved project objective. That discovery might suggest that an important objective was omitted as the project was planned and that the project's objectives should be readdressed.

Each test case identified for a project should tie directly to an approved project requirement. Training needs and user manual content should likewise trace to user

FIGURE 4.10 Simple Project Status Report Template

Client			
Project Name		**Date of Report**	
Tasks Completed this Period			
Tasks Scheduled for Next Period			
Outstanding Issues			
Issues for Senior Management Action		**Point of Contact**	

requirements. In every instance, what is to be purchased, built, integrated, tested, trained, and documented should trace to the approved requirements specification (Figure 4.11). Requirements traceability enables the project team to ensure that the full project scope has been designed into, developed, and tested for a technical solution.

FIGURE 4.11 Requirements Traceability Template

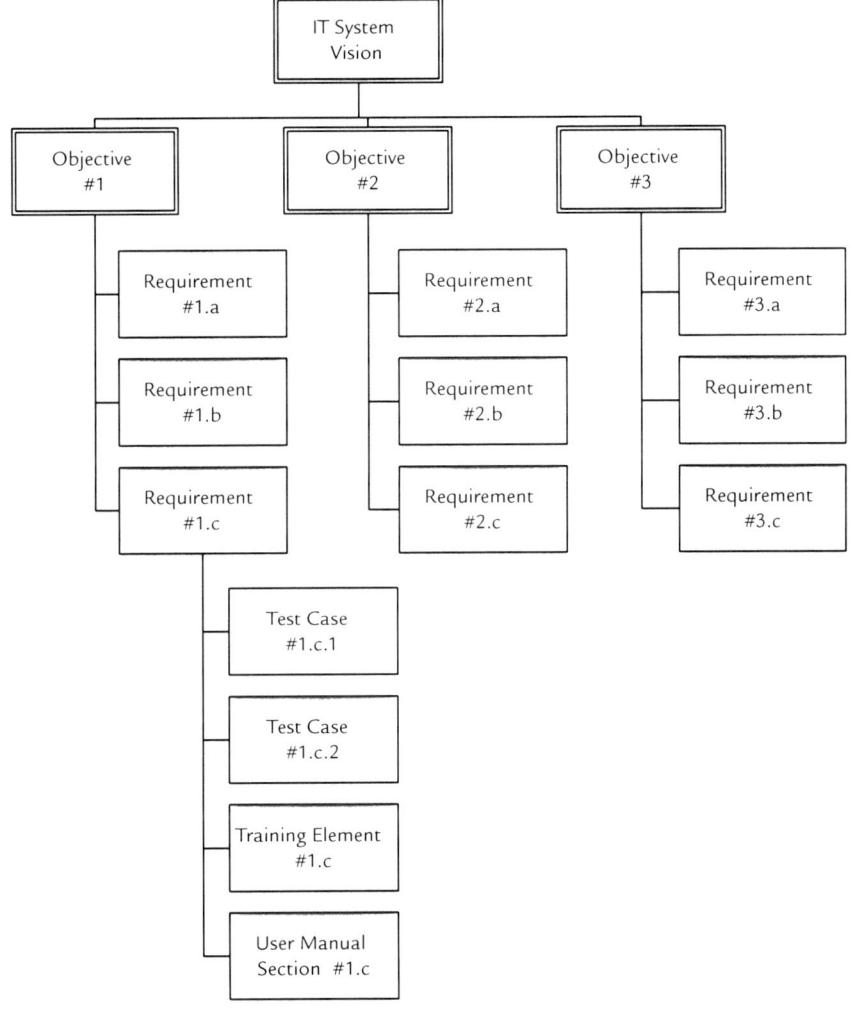

Q11 What role does business analysis have in the planning process?

Business analysis is the discipline that defines, models, and documents the business processes that are to be supported by an IT solution. It translates those processes into documentation that technical staff can use to construct an acceptable IT solution. The products of business analysis include business process descriptions, workflow diagrams, data models, use cases, and data migration requirements that the project team can use to fulfill a need for a new or updated IT system.

The prospect of a new or updated system provides a great opportunity to rethink how business is being done in an organization. The business analyst can be a great resource in carrying out that process. Too often business processes are shaped around the limitations and capabilities of the IT system currently used to support those processes. It is the responsibility of the business analysts to see beyond the limitations of the current state of business and facilitate user thinking that drives the new system more closely to a user's desired state, where increased efficiency and effectiveness are possible.

Q12 What risks should be considered when planning an IT project?

A risk identifies the likelihood of something happening that could impact the project. Risks can be positive or negative. Negative risks, if manifest, could hurt the project; positive risks, if they occur, have a positive impact.

IT projects often take technology in new directions or apply it in ways never attempted prior to the project. Going where no one has gone before entails a fair amount of risk, and the wise project manager identifies potential risks proactively.

Common risks found in IT projects are identified in Figure 4.12. Note how few of the risks relate to technology. IT projects, like most types of projects, are carried out by people. People are the source of most of the risks likely to be experienced on an IT project.

FIGURE 4.12 Common IT Project Risks

Description	Strategy
Transfer System Code Conversion Task Complexity It is probable that the complexity of the conversion process for the code has been understated.	*Mitigate the risk.* Gather legacy system documentation and distribute it to the contractors to help them understand the complexity of the systems.
Requirements Management Plans currently in place to capture the details of the system requirements are not adequate. This might result in the loss of important details as people transition to other jobs and leave the organization, losing the information. This could later result in rework, impacting project cost and schedule for Phase 2.	*Avoid the risk.* • Develop a requirements management plan to address the need to capture requirements as they are presented. • Establish procedures for capturing, documenting, and detailing user-suggested system enhancements now.

Requirements Management Plans currently in place to capture the details of the system requirements are not adequate. This might result in the loss of important details as people transition to other jobs and leave the organization, losing the information. This could later result in rework, impacting project cost and schedule for Phase 2.	*Avoid the risk.* • Develop a requirements management plan to address the need to capture requirements as they are presented. • Establish procedures for capturing, documenting, and detailing user-suggested system enhancements now.
Comprehensive Testing As the project moves into the later phases of the schedule, comprehensive testing assumes a greater level of importance to the project. There is a tendency in all projects to move ahead too fast once a significant milestone has been achieved. However, there is no guarantee at that time that the code is fully operational—only that it loads and compiles as required. Comprehensive testing remains a key to ensuring the final system produced by the project is acceptable.	*Avoid the risk.* • Ensure plans for thorough testing of the code are preserved and that rework is completed as necessary. • As enhancements to the code are identified, approved, designed, and developed, engage users early and often for testing to ensure the acceptability of the modifications.
Configuration Management There is a possibility that the vendor will continue to modify the code throughout the life of the project. This will create a complex configuration management challenge that, if not controlled, will affect both the cost of the project and the ability to deliver the project on schedule.	*Avoid the risk.* • Develop a comprehensive configuration management (CM) plan that addresses integration, management, and release of the code as modifications are made. • Carefully track the state of the code, including versioning and ownership of changes. This strategy is in process by the project manager.
Schedule Management Significant slips in schedule are commonly experienced on IT projects. Although these slips might not significantly affect the organization's ability to complete the system on schedule, the team's ability to successfully complete system testing and move through the project is often overestimated.	*Mitigate the risk.* • Review scheduled project tasks in light of the apparent schedule variances. • Re-baseline the project schedule and revisit expectations for the project in terms of testing and acceptance of the re-hosted system, along with the goals and objectives for the project.

(continued)

(continued)

Description	Strategy
User Involvement The development methodology has not included input from the business users on the team. Input has been provided primarily by the project manager and technical resources. Given that workflow, business rules, processes, and data requirements are being interpreted by the integrator, the absence of business input poses a significant risk that may affect schedule and cost if rework is required later as a result of this oversight. Scope may also be increased without the benefit of input from users who can confirm what is actually in scope and what is not, as the integrator continues the development process.	*Mitigate the impact.* Involve users early and often in the development process. Have business users review workflows, business rules, and data structures that have been developed by the integration team to validate their accuracy and correct them as needed.
Schedule Management Updated schedules remain overly fluid for the project. This results from the continuing levels of unanticipated complexity encountered by the project team. This might result in a tendency to abbreviate testing. The lack of thorough testing—both user-based and system testing—might cause the project to be extended beyond the currently projected end date so that system bugs can be resolved. If realized, the impact of this risk might also be felt in terms of increased cost to do rework, and potential system failure.	*Mitigate the risk.* The project manager should continue to manage the project schedule closely and provide periodic appraisals of project progress to the project sponsor and Steering Committee.
Budget The current budget burn rate for the project's budget, as reported by the project manager, suggests that the remaining budget might not be sufficient to complete the project unless extreme discipline is applied by the project management team and contractor. This risk would manifest as a possible budget overrun.	*Mitigate the risk.* The project team, led by the project manager, should monitor the project budget to manage this risk. Budget reviews should be completed on a regular basis to ensure that trends that might be used to identify potential problems are recognized well in advance of the need for specific action.

Mature Methodology As a result of schedule and budget shortfalls, along with unanticipated complexity within the development process, testing has been abbreviated. This action might impact cost, schedule, and scope if testing is not adequate and avoidable rework is encountered. Scope could be compromised as well if a module is not sufficiently tested from the system's perspective and fails as a result of system stress or bulk load issues.	*Mitigate the risk.* - Conduct a comprehensive review of each module of the system before deployment to ensure that the business staff, technical staff, and contractor are satisfied that testing has been adequate prior to cutover of the new systems. - Require that a readiness assessment be completed and signed off by the contractor, project manager, and technical lead prior to acceptance of the system. Require written acceptance of the system by the project sponsor before any portion of the system is put online.
Management Involvement With increasing need by senior management to tend to ongoing operations, their involvement in the project might be diminished. If this situation persists and the team is not allowed to benefit from direct interaction with senior management, project success could be threatened as the team wrestles with short schedules, budgets, and conflicting perceptions about project scope.	*Mitigate the risk.* Consider changing meeting times and using alternative means of communications to ensure senior management remains engaged and that the team has access to direct and timely feedback.
Budget Management The time and materials nature of any contract offers the potential for scope creep. This has the potential to allow the contractor to drive scope, impacting schedule and cost.	*Mitigate the impact.* - Require the contractor to develop discrete estimates for specific pieces of work that have been scoped in detail, including a clear statement of what will be developed, the cost and schedule, and how the client will confirm that the tasks have been completed. - Incorporate go/no go checkpoints based on both cost and schedule, for monitoring contractor performance. - Require formal acceptance of each piece of work completed by the contractor.

(continues)

(continued)

Description	Strategy
User Involvement	*Mitigate the risk.*
A key member of the business team might leave the project at a key point in time. This person has a significant role in interpreting business requirements, communicating with stakeholders, and validating that the developers have appropriately interpreted business requirements. The loss of this person is likely to impact the ability of the development team to accurately interpret and deliver functional requirements and ultimately to deliver the project's scope.	Early in the project, identify a backup resource that can assist the project's development team in interpreting requirements and take the lead when the departing resource is no longer available.

DELIVERABLES

Q1 What deliverables are typically generated during the project planning process?

The bulk of a project's deliverables come from the planning phase of a project, which is when the team develops the detailed plans and specifications for the project.

Think of what it takes to plan a week-long backpacking excursion into the mountains. The hikers lay out a clear path from the starting point to the destination, using a map. They identify the people going on the hike and the equipment and supplies the group might need for the trip. Then they meet to get organized.

Planning an IT project follows pretty much the same process. The plan lays out the path from the starting point to the destination. The deliverables lay out that path and the boundaries within which the project team follows and observes. Once the project's path is known, the deliverables make it possible to track the project's progress from planning to project closeout.

Typical deliverables generated during the planning process of an IT project are listed in Figure 4.13.

There is no end to the number of documents and specifications potentially developed for an IT project during the planning process. More than one IT project has been planned to death, exhausting its budget and schedule through obsessive planning and generation of documents that extended beyond the point of need. The rule of thumb for exactly how much planning and how many deliverables are required for a project is:

FIGURE 4.13 Planning Process Deliverables

Deliverable Title	Deliverable Title
Integrated project management plan	Procurement management plan
Scope management plan	System implementation plan
Change management plan	Project schedule
Schedule management plan	Detailed statement of scope
Cost management plan	System requirements specification
Configuration management plan	Technical requirements specification
Issues management plan	System architecture
Resource management plan	Network diagrams
Quality management plan	Test case documentation
Communications management plan	Test management plan
Requirements management plan	Unit test plan
Risk management plan	Systems test plan
Human resource management plan	Integration test plan
Staff management plan	Deliverable acceptance documentation
Performance test plan	Project closeout report
User acceptance test plan	Lessons learned report
Test results documentation	Request for information
Request for proposal	

Minimum effort/maximum gain: Generate the minimum number of deliverables necessary to provide the maximum benefit to the project.

For every potential deliverable generated during the planning phase, the project manager should be able to clearly articulate the benefit the item will provide to the project. If no clear benefit can be identified, the deliverable should be deleted from the project effort.

Q2 What level of detail do you need when identifying new system requirements?

The rule for developing requirements for an IT project is to define them to the level of detail necessary to estimate the work.

Requirements are the things built to satisfy the objectives of the project. Project objectives describe the value the project will provide to the business. Objectives are written statements that are SMART—Specific, Measurable, Assignable to one or more stakeholders, Realistic, and Time-bound.

Requirements spring directly from objectives. Requirements are things, rather than work. A user interface is a requirement. A database is a requirement. A specific report is a requirement.

Building the database is an activity or task, which is not to be confused with a requirement. Building the user interface also is an activity or task.

Activities and tasks are the work done to build the requirements. The goal in defining requirements is to get to the level of detail at which the team can estimate the amount and nature of the tasks required to satisfy the requirements.

Take the example of a project to build a new financial accounting system that includes accounts payable, accounts receivable, a general ledger, and a grants management module that will help manage gifts of money given to the organization for specific purposes. When defining the requirements for the new system, the team may list the accounts payable subsystem and accounts payable subsystem as requirements and go no further in terms of detail. Having done a number of finance and accounting systems, the team realizes that accounts payable and accounts receivable functions are generally the same, no matter what type of business they are used for. They realize that they can purchase commercial off-the-shelf solutions for accounts receivable and accounts payable and integrate them with the overall system with little difficulty. Beyond that, they require no more detail to understand what is needed to satisfy the client's needs.

On the other hand, the team also knows that the requirement for a general ledger might be a bit more specific to the business. Organizations often tailor their general ledger subsystems to meet the unique needs of the organization. The functionality of a general ledger does not tend to change very much from financial system implementation to financial system implementation, but the context in which the company applies it may take a bit more detail to appreciate. In this instance, the team can define the general ledger requirements to some level of detail before they are satisfied that they understand the client's needs.

Grant management systems can be unique, and they often vary substantially from business to business and system to system. Appreciating that, a project team should know from the onset that they will need to define the requirements for the grants subsystem to a greater level of detail than the accounts payable, accounts receivable, or general ledger system before they can appreciate the details of what needs to be constructed.

In the end, the level of detail defined for any project depends on what the client wants in the system, how familiar the team is with the things the client wants, and how generic or unique those requirements might be. For any single software development or integration project, the level of detail to which requirements are defined varies from requirement to requirement (Figure 4.14).

FIGURE 4.14 Sample Detailed Requirements in Conceptual View

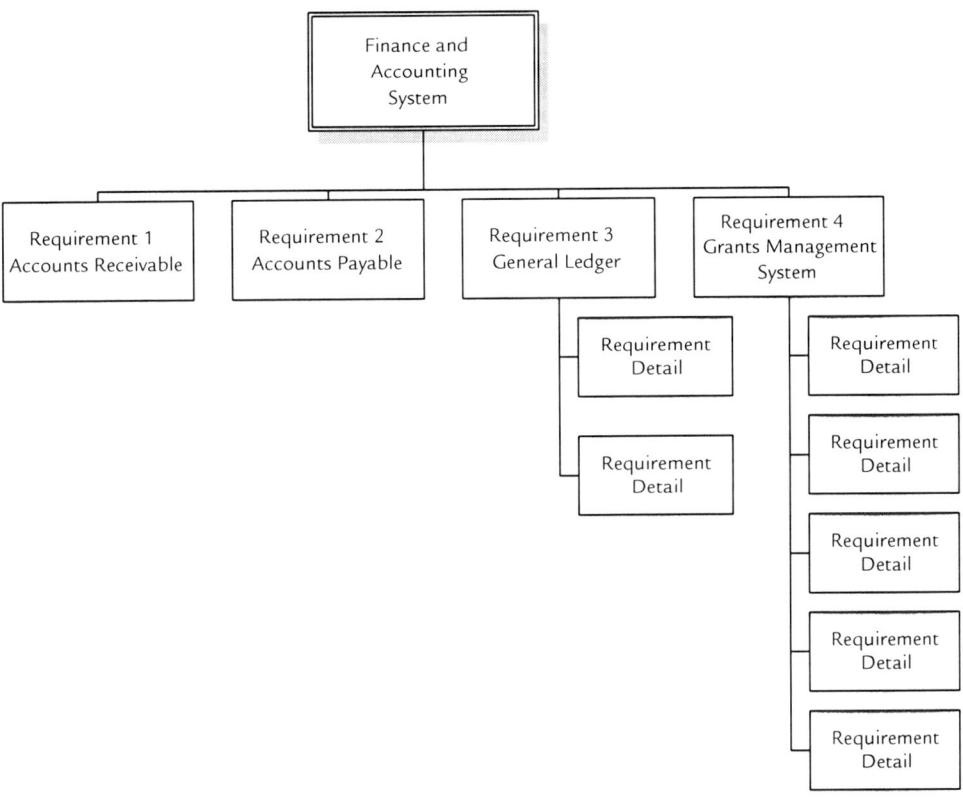

Q3 What is included in a project management plan for an IT project?

A project plan can be as long or as short as is needed to support an IT project. If an IT project can be completed in a couple of days by a few people and carries little risk, plan it on a piece of scratch paper. Larger projects usually require more.

Figure 4.15 identifies the common elements of a project management plan for an IT project in checklist form.

FIGURE 4.15 Project Management Plan Development Checklist

Integrated Project Management Plan Content	Included: Yes/No/NA
1. Purpose	
2. Audience	

(continues)

(continued)

Integrated Project Management Plan Content	Included: Yes/No/NA
3. Project scope	
a. Summary of business case	
b. Inclusions	
c. Exclusions	
4. Criteria for success	
5. Assumptions and constraints	
6. Project deliverables and deliverables management requirements	
a. List of major deliverables for the project	
b. Roles and responsibilities for deliverables	
i. Project manager	
ii. Executive steering committee	
iii. Executive sponsor	
iv. Core team members	
v. Vendor project manager	
vi. Project team membership	
vii. Other	
7. Project governance/roles and responsibilities	
a. Project sponsor	
b. Project steering committee membership	
c. Project managers	
d. Core team	
e. Vendor project team	
f. Subject matter experts	
g. Other	
8. Project budget	
a. Budget summary	
b. Assumptions	
9. Work plan/schedule	

a. Overview of project approach	
b. Project work plan	
c. Project initiation activities	
d. Project planning activities	
e. Project control activities	
f. Project execution activities	
g. Project closeout activities	
10. Project schedule	
a. Project timeline	
b. Key milestones	
11. Integrated plans	
a. Risk management plan	
b. Issue management plan	
c. Communications plan	
d. Stakeholder management analysis and plan	
e. Budget management plan	
f. Scope/change management plan	
g. Quality management plan	
h. Quality assurance plan	
i. Contractor management plan	
j. Schedule management plan	
k. Staffing plan	
l. Acquisition plan/procurement management	
m. Test plan	
n. Training plan	
o. Implementation and transition	
p. Data integration/migration	
q. Other	
12. Other	

TEST PLANNING

Q1 What is unit testing?

Units are the building blocks of a software application. A unit is one single object or module of a system. Potential units include a set of code that calls a printer or renders a user interface screen.

Unit testing is carried out by the developers of the code. Test cases completed by the developers are documented by project analysts before the code is developed so that the test cases can be used as a guide for the software developers. Once unit testing has been completed successfully, the unit of code is provided to the project's configuration manager for inclusion in a future build of the new or modified system.

Q2 What is system testing?

During system testing, a single subsystem of a software application is tested as a stand-alone element of an entire system, prior to integration with other subsystems. System testing ensures that the subsystem fulfills the user's needs as specified in the approved requirements list for the project.

System testing is accomplished using test cases that simulate actual business processes. The data used for a system test is generally made available through a simple device such as a spreadsheet or database, constructed specifically to support the test scenario.

Interfaces with other systems are not tested beyond the boundary of the subsystem. Test cases for system testing are provided by business and technical analysts assigned to the project, and they are coordinated by the project's test manager.

Q3 What is integration testing?

System testing precedes integration and performance testing. During integration and performance testing, numerous subsystems are brought together and integrated. The goal is to test the aggregation of subsystems to determine whether they will function as specified, as a collective set of software.

Interfaces with other systems are not tested beyond the boundary of the specific subsystems identified for integration and testing. The test cases for integration testing are generally the same test cases used for unit testing and system testing. The project's business and technical analysts provide them.

Parallel testing may be incorporated into integration and performance testing. In those instances, similar test cases are run against the integrated subsystems and the legacy system that is to be replaced. A comparison of the results from the parallel testing confirms whether the new system works as anticipated.

Q4 What is performance testing?

Performance tests are carried out to verify that performance requirements specified for the system can be met. The measurement used to confirm the success or failure of this test is most often referred to as response time. Performance testing is usually conducted during integration testing to ensure the subsystems that have been integrated for testing perform as specified. However, performance testing may be completed as a separate testing activity.

Automated tools are often used to complete performance testing. Such tools may measure user interface refresh rates, bandwidth consumed by a new system, and data accuracy during the data migration process.

Q5 What is user acceptance testing?

User acceptance testing (UAT) is the last, best chance for the project team and the system users to ensure a system is ready for acceptance and fit for use.

UAT is generally managed by the project's test manager and executed by a test team. The test team may be composed of those people who will ultimately rely on the new or upgraded system to complete their daily business, as well as those who must support and maintain the system once it is in production.

UAT should follow formal training of the system's users so that they are well prepared to exercise the new system during testing. User manuals and system maintenance documentation should be in draft form, at least, prior to UAT. This enables the users and technical staff to test the efficacy of the training and the accuracy of the new system's documentation as a part of testing.

UAT is guided by the same test cases that were developed and used during unit testing, system testing, integration testing, and performance testing. Test cases should trace directly to the approved requirements specifications for the project and ensure that all priority requirements are thoroughly exercised by the test team. Once UAT has been completed, the system is ready for final readiness assessment and potential acceptance.

Q6 What is regression testing?

During the course of any test process, defects that require rework of some major or minor components of the system might be identified. When this occurs, a decision must be made as to whether the rework potentially threatens the integrity of the rest of the system. If a new piece of code or change to the database potentially impacts major portions of the system, it is often prudent to "regress" and run through the entire test scenario again from the beginning. During regression testing, the test team repeats all the test cases leading up to and including the area of the system that was reworked.

Regression testing can be very expensive. It should be conducted only when absolutely necessary to ensure the integrity of the system.

Q7 What documentation needs to be produced during and after testing?

Test results should be compiled and reviewed by the project team during and after each phase of testing on an IT project. The simple rule is that if you can't prove a system requirement was tested, it is best to assume it was not tested at all.

Test documentation should identify each test case addressed during testing. Each test case should cross-reference to the requirements specified for the project from which the test case was derived. The results of the tester's assessment of the test case should be annotated in the results, identifying whether the system produced the anticipated result. If the result was less than that anticipated, the test results should identify the corrective action taken to remedy the situation.

The test manager and test team review all test results during testing and at the conclusion of the test process. Once the review has been completed, the test manager recommends to the project manager and project sponsor whether the test results should be accepted. The project sponsor generally signs a deliverable acceptance document, indicating that the tests were completed to his satisfaction, based on that recommendation.

Acceptance of the test results of any phase of testing above the unit test level constitutes an exit gate for that testing and entrance criteria for the next phase of testing.

DATABASE DESIGN

Q1 How do you organize database development during the planning phase?

Database development is carried out best by resources trained in the discipline of database modeling. Too often the task is left up to software developers who have little understanding of how databases are constructed. The result is inefficient and inflexible systems.

Project managers should ensure that their projects benefit from the experience and training of a skilled database modeler whenever possible. They should also plan for collaboration between the software development team and the project's data modelers to ensure that the database is constructed with sufficient clarity and logic to support the system's needs.

Users should be directly involved with database development. They should not be excluded from the process even though they might lack the technical background to construct a database. In fact, if a nontechnical person is walked through the database model for the new system, understands it, and agrees that it will adequately support his business needs, the chance of user acceptance of the system is greatly improved.

During a recent project, system developers had constructed a database to support a system that apportions a state's tax dollars to individual school districts. A quality assurance review of the database suggested that the database model did not adequately reflect the user's needs for access to specific types of data. The quality assurance analyst suggested that the database modelers and the users meet and walk through the database design together to resolve the situation.

At first, the technical staff balked at the prospect of working with nontechnical resources to review the database. The business-oriented system users protested that they could not possibly contribute to the design because they lacked a technical background. The project sponsor directed that the review be conducted regardless.

The database review was conducted. It lasted several hours, as the technical staff laboriously explained their design in nontechnical terms and the users attempted to understand the explanations. Several times, discussions nearly broke down as both sides attempted to translate tech-speak into lay terms. They persisted nonetheless, and when the review was finally completed, the team emerged with a joint appreciation of the project's needs.

The outcome of the process included an upgraded database design that both the database modeler and business staff felt was much improved. The business users left the review with heightened confidence that the technical staff had designed a system that would indeed meet their needs. The organization that conducted the project now incorporates user reviews of database designs as a standard practice for all software development projects.

Q2 What is database modeling?

Database modeling organizes the data needs of a business unit, in as efficient a manner as possible, to support the functionality of an automated system. Data modeling should be accomplished by trained database modelers whenever possible.

The modeling process includes several versions of database designs:

- *Conceptual data model*—Depicts high-level entities within the data
- *Logical data model*—Identifies data entities to a detailed level, including all the significant attributes of each entity and its relationship to other entities within the model
- *Physical database*—The actual database design in final form.

These different constructs of the database model allow a project team to work from a simple concept through construction of the actual database. They enable the project team to logically progress from a conceptual idea of how a project's data should be organized through to the point where the actual storage and accessibility of that data can be defined in detail and converted into an aspect of a functioning system.

The various forms of database models include progressing from least to greatest degree of granularity, the conceptual data model, the logical data model, and the physical database.

Q3 What is a conceptual data model?

A conceptual data model is one that identifies all the major entities to be included in a database model. No attempt is made to define those entities to any detailed level.

A conceptual data model depicts the major entities that will be included in the database from a business process level. It provides the first view of how the technical team envisions the database, given the requirements documented for the project; how users have expressed their needs during interviews, and so on. The conceptual data model can be reviewed with the future system users to ensure the model captures their needs.

The sample conceptual model provided in Figure 4.16 depicts high-level entities. It represents a typical simplified security model for an application. The user entity represents the person logging on to a system, who can be assigned to one or more roles and to one or more groups.

FIGURE 4.16 Simple Conceptual Data Model

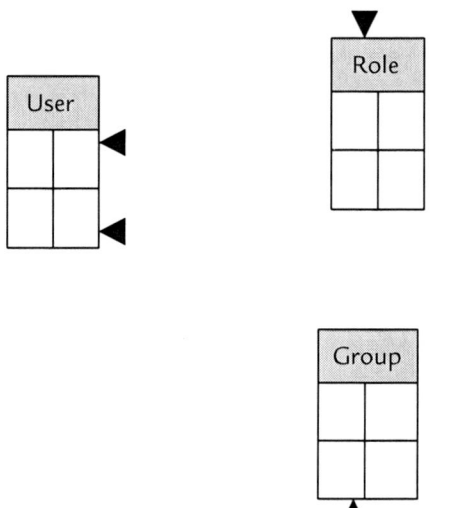

Q4 What is a logical data model?

The logical data model elaborates on the conceptual data model. It includes more detail, including the model attributes and the associate entities (bridge tables/entities) that are generally not shown in the conceptual business model. Entities are identified in table form, including much of the detail that describes the data associated with each entity. The relationships between entities are clearly articulated. Entities are decomposed to the point where they logically need not be defined further to be accessed and used by the system's software.

In Figure 4.17, the business model has been updated to provide more detail around primary keys and foreign keys, as well as to show the actual table names. The entities are prefixed with "sec" to identify security entities and remove ambiguity between users, where a similar entity might also appear in the model.

FIGURE 4.17 Logical Data Model

sec_User		sec_User_Element		sec_Element		sec_Dimension	
PK	Id	PK	Id	PK	Id	PK	Id
	UserName				Code		Name
	FName	FK2	User_Id	FK1	Dimension_Id		Code
	LName	FK1	Element_Id		Name		
					Type		

The logical data model forms the basis of the physical data model, used as an aspect of the final system design and construct.

Q5 What is a physical database?

The physical database is an elaboration of the logical data model. It is constructed and used as an integral element of the deliverable technical solution. The physical database creates the capability to receive, store, and make accessible the data required by the system's users.

Chapter 5

PROJECT EXECUTION

The project execution process puts the detailed project plans developed by the project team into motion. The time for focusing on identifying requirements, detailing processes, creating designs, and positioning the team to produce the deliverable technical solution is substantially complete. Although the process of progressively elaborating those requirements, processes, designs, and team assignments will almost certainly continue to some extent through the life of the project, the execution process shifts the focus of the project toward using those project artifacts to bring the project's products to life.

The vast majority of a project's time and money is consumed during the execution process. All effort up to this point has involved thoughtful consideration, intellectual deliberation, and careful crafting of project documentation. Once the team moves into execution, the pressure is on to produce something tangible. When the execution process is complete and a solution has been provided to the user, the lion's share of the work is done for the project team. It is a time of great accomplishment but also a time of great risk.

PROJECT MANAGEMENT CONSIDERATIONS

Q1 When does project planning end and project execution begin?

The exit criterion for project planning includes the completion of the project's detailed project planning document, the project management plan. What that document contains is unique to each project, but once the plan is done, the project's approach to providing the deliverable technical solution should be well understood.

There's an old project management adage that says, "Never be afraid to replan." Change happens, and project plans must be flexible and updated through the course of the entire project management life cycle. From that perspective, project planning never ends. It starts once an IT project is chartered and continues to the end of the project.

It is convenient to think of the life cycle of an IT project as linear, with clear starting points and ending points as one phase ends and another begins. That, however, is not how it works in reality.

Because so many IT projects plow new ground for the business world, it is nearly impossible to fully understand a project's requirements until it is actually underway. Successful IT project managers understand that, at best, they will be able to plan 80 to 85 percent of a project with some confidence; the rest will be discovered along the way, during project execution.

Q2 Who leads the project execution effort?

The project sponsor is the project's de facto leader. It is that person who champions the project within the organization and ensures that the project manager has sufficient resources to carry the project through to completion.

From the project management perspective, there is only one hands-on leader for any project, and that is the project manager. That position is formalized by the project sponsor's signature of the project charter during the project's initiation phase. Other members of the project team may appropriately take up the project's leadership mantle on occasion, but the responsibility for leadership of the project team fundamentally rests with one person alone—the project manager.

Leadership can be defined as the ability to get people to do things that they might not normally do on their own and understand the value. Good leaders and effective project managers gain the commitment of the team members. They lead through the expression of their professional knowledge, communication skills, empathy, charisma, technical expertise, and project management expertise.

Good leaders also know when to surrender leadership. There are times when the most important factor at play on a project is the leader's ability to recognize when skilled project management is the dominant need of the moment, and the project manager takes charge. As the project moves into a technical phase of the effort, however, the project manager might step aside and focus the limelight on the team's technical lead or architect. Another day, it might be the business team lead, communications manager, or test manager who offers the leadership the team needs to carry the project forward. In each case, a good project manager knows when to step aside and surrender leadership to a more appropriate member of the team and when it is time to take it back again.

Q3 What events are commonly tracked during the project execution process?

Project execution can consume up to 60 percent of a project's schedule and budget. The work described in the detailed project plans is undertaken during this phase. The number and type of tasks can be extensive.

Figure 5.1 provides an excellent checklist of items to monitor during the course of project execution.

FIGURE 5.1 Project Execution Checklist

Project Execution Event Checklist	Yes/No/NA
1. Is progress tracked against the budget?	
2. Is there a baselined schedule with identified milestones?	
3. Is progress tracked against the schedule?	
4. Are requirements routinely validated against test results?	
5. Is status submitted to the project sponsor on a regular basis?	
6. Are project team meetings held regularly?	
7. Are issues recorded and tracked to resolution?	
8. Are changes managed using a change management plan?	
9. Do all team members understand and use the project plan?	
10. Do team members understand their roles and lines of communication?	
11. Do the client's expectations match those of the contractor?	
12. Are deliverables scheduled appropriately?	
a. Assign a resource	
b. Produce the deliverable	
c. Content validation	
d. Rework	
e. Production	
f. Draft submission	
g. Client comment period	

(continues)

(continued)

Project Execution Event Checklist	Yes/No/NA
h. Rework	
i. Final production	
j. Final quality assurance	
k. Delivery	
13. Has the acceptance criteria been clearly stated and tied to project completion?	
14. Has the design–test process been executed using best practices, including:	
a. *Business design*	
i. Sequence diagrams	
ii. User interface standard for project	
iii. Mapping of user interface	
iv. User interface screens	
v. Design notes	
a. *Technical requirements*	
i. Programming methodology, e.g., ASP over COM	
ii. Software	
iii. Client requirements	
iv. Server requirements	
v. Communication	
vi. Versions	
vii. Hardware	
1. Client	
2. Server	
b. *Development*	
i. Security	
ii. Backups	
iii. Deployment/build	

iv. System failure mechanism (business resumption)	
v. System release method	
vi. Source control	
vii. Database transaction method	
viii. Interface Specifications	
c. *Technical design*	
i. Logical data model	
ii. Class diagrams	
iii. Detail sequence diagrams/collaboration of objects	
iv. Stored procedures	
v. Design notes	
vi. Standards for coding	
vii. Technical guidelines	
d. *Testing*	
i. Test plan/scripts	
ii. Unit testing	
iii. Functional	
iv. Integration	
v. Stress	
e. *Readiness assessment*	
i. Communications	
ii. Network	
iii. Training	
iv. Manual availability	
v. Hardware	
vi. Go/no go decision	
15. Has the project been signed off as accepted by the project sponsor?	

Q4 How frequently should the users be involved during execution of an IT project?

As was the case during the project planning process, users should be involved early and often during the course of project execution. There are too many cases of projects where a team constructed an elegant technical solution for an organization only to have it rejected by the users. The organization's investment in the project was lost, and the project team's efforts were wasted.

It is not always easy to decipher the user's requirements or desires for a new system. The technical team invariably comes up with a host of questions in that regard. The users usually have the answers to those questions. It takes excellent communication skills on both sides of the discussion to ensure that the user's lay perspective is converted into language the technical team can implement. Where those communication skills come up lacking, an experienced business analyst can often fill the void.

Q5 What is independent verification and validation?

Independent verification and validation (IV&V) is a quality assurance approach that helps the project management team ensure a project is planned and executed as intended.

An IV&V team consists of technical and nontechnical resources acquired from outside the organization. The team provides an objective review of the project, from vision to technical architecture, through the execution process. Emphasis is placed on configuration management and requirements traceability to ensure that every deliverable is provided in accordance with specification and that every specification supports the project sponsor's vision and objectives.

IV&V goes beyond normal project quality assurance efforts. Project quality assurance focuses on how a project is managed, and whether project management best practices are in place and implemented by the project team. IV&V digs deeper into the project's specifications to ensure that each element of a specification aligns with an approved project requirement and that all specifications have been met when the final product is delivered.

When a project is highly complex, IV&V provides assurances to the project manager and project sponsor that every requirement has been addressed appropriately. It is not recommended for every project because of its potentially high cost. It might not be required where the project team has a good record of delivering successful projects, the sponsoring organization has demonstrated a high level of project management maturity, or the project's objectives and requirements pose little risk to the project.

Q6 Who should approve technical design documents?

The project sponsor has ultimate responsibility for approval of any deliverable developed by the project team. The project sponsor authorizes and pays for the project and is accountable to the organization for the project's success. However, it is unrealistic to expect a project sponsor, who has myriad other duties within the business, to personally sign off on every report, design document, database model, or architectural diagram generated by the team. On the other hand, the project manager has overall responsibility for the day-to-day activities of the project team. From that standpoint, who is in charge when it comes to approving technical design documents for an IT project?

There is no rule regarding who approves any specific deliverable developed by a project team. It makes sense, however, that the person with the best technical eye for the details involved in a technical design should be delegated responsibility for reviewing and accepting that design.

Some time ago, a produce inspection system was constructed for a large state agriculture agency. The system architecture was developed for the new system, which included hard-coding the system's security into the code written by the software developer. That approach was written into the architectural design document by the project's technical architect and approved by that same person without further review.

Well after much of the new system's software had been coded, the project manager requested an external architectural review by another technical architect not involved in the project. The technical architect uncovered the hard-coded security model and designated it an inappropriate design. Unfortunately, the project team had completed the code for that area of the system some months before the review.

The project team redesigned and reworked the security module of the system to comply with the external reviewer's findings. The error in the system was corrected, but not before the software development company expended over $40,000 in developer costs and two weeks of effort. The team consumed an equivalent amount of time and money implementing a table-driven security model, which provided the client a much easier platform for managing system security.

In this instance, the project team had not adequately addressed the design review process. The project would have benefited from external review and approval by someone other than the project's technical architect much earlier in the process of design and execution.

Project design documents should be reviewed and approved by the project resource best qualified to do those reviews. However, no single project resource—no matter how well qualified—should be held accountable for reviewing and approving his own design documents.

Q7 What is project control and why is it important during the execution process?

A project manager with control over a projects knows where she planned for the project to be at any point in the project, knows with some certainty where the project actually is at that point in time, and has the ability to influence the difference.

Contrary to popular belief, control is not about being an autocrat or dictator, or manipulating people's actions. Control involves knowing your project inside and out, being able to prove where your project is at any point in time, and managing the challenges.

Some years ago, a project sponsor called a quality assurance analyst into her office to observe a meeting with a young project manager. When the project manager entered the sponsor's office, the sponsor asked him to provide a status of the project. The project manager replied, "The project is about 50 percent done and has spent only a little of its contingency budget. It is in very good shape."

The project sponsor asked the project manager to step outside the office and then asked the quality assurance analyst for advice. "I have no idea what he means when he says the project is 50 percent done, and I have no idea if using some of the project's contingency is good or bad. What can I do?"

The analyst replied, "Tell him to prove it. When it comes to IT projects, a subjective assessment of the project's status is not good enough. You need an objective assessment of the project—something he can prove beyond a reasonable doubt, which you can rely on."

The sponsor called the project manager back into her office and put the question to him. She gave him three days to report back with the project's status. Three days later, the project manager showed up at the sponsor's office. He had not left the building during that period. Instead, he had spent the time at his desk with his project team, constructing and updating a project schedule that should have existed before. He had developed a definitive list of deliverables for the project and identified which had been delivered and accepted by the project team and which remained to be completed. He had validated the project's expenditures to date. It took a full three days of concerted effort, around the clock, to reconstruct that information.

Amazingly, the upshot of his efforts was that when he reported back to the project sponsor, it was true that approximately 50 percent of the project was complete. Some contingency budget had been applied to specific tasks, in a reasonable and effective manner. A little digging showed that the project manager's positive outcome turned out to be due more to the diligence of his team members, who were informally keeping track of the project, than to any effort on his part.

This project manager was lucky. He had lost control over his project. If his project team had not been doing such a good job in spite of him, he could have lost his job. As it was, he spent three frantic days trying to determine what he should have known all along. It was a great lesson for both the project manager and the project sponsor.

When you manage an IT project, money and expectations are on the line. Your project sponsor and stakeholder expect you to maintain control over your project. That does not mean that your team members jump to your every command. It means that you know what is going on with your project at all times. When you say that the project is about 50 percent complete and in great shape, you and your project sponsor have confidence that your assessment is based on solid evidence. You can prove it. You know where you planned to be, can objectively determine where you actually are, and are in a good position to influence the difference.

Q8 How often should project team meetings be held?

Talk to any project team member, and he is likely to tell you that the key to a good project is to have as few team meetings as possible; the fewer the number of meetings, the more time the team members have to implement the project's design.

On some projects, there are so many meetings that it is hard to figure out when anyone has time to get any real work accomplished. On other projects, there is so little communication between team members that no one seems to know what is going on. A happy medium does exist. Adhere to the following rules for conducting project team meetings and you will reach a happy medium, where meetings are tolerable and productive and the project team has time to do their work.

- Rule #1: Hold the minimum number of meetings necessary to provide the maximum benefit for the project. If you can't specify the benefit a meeting will provide to the project, don't hold the meeting.
- Rule #2: Hold regularly scheduled meetings if something important needs to be discussed or a decision needs to be made. If not, cancel the meeting. People will thank you for freeing up a little time in their otherwise busy schedules.
- Rule #3: If you can take care of the items on a meeting's agenda on a one-on-one basis with the potential attendees, do so rather than hold the meeting. Otherwise, you are wasting the other attendees' time, and they will be reluctant to support your meetings in the future.
- Rule #4: With the exception of workshops, never hold a meeting that lasts more than 60 minutes. The old adage that the brain can manage what the posterior can tolerate is all too true. After about an hour of sitting in one place, people become distracted and start thinking about the work piling up on their desks. When they lose their focus, the meeting loses its value. For a workshop that

might require half a day or more, consider breaking the workshop into one-hour sessions to give attendees a break. Your chances of achieving a productive outcome will be much improved.

- Rule #5: Always have an agenda. Publish the agenda well in advance so that attendees have adequate time to prepare. That sets their expectations for a productive, focused working session and allows them to bow out of the meeting if it does not involve them.
- Rule #6: Once a meeting starts, stick to the agenda. An agenda is a contract with the meeting's attendees. It sets their expectations for what will be addressed, their level of involvement, and how long the meeting will last. How much they contribute during the meeting and how satisfied they are when it is over depend upon how well you meet those expectations, and your agenda is a great tool in that regard.

Q9 What types of meetings are commonly held during IT projects?

A list of the more common meetings held to support an IT project is provided in Figure 5.2.

FIGURE 5.2 Project Meetings

Meeting	Description	Normal Frequency	Normal Duration
Project team	All members of the project team are brought together to receive an overview of the project status and future assignments, and to discuss project risks, issues, and change requests. Scheduled and led by the project manager.	Monthly	≤1 hour
Individual project team member update	Meetings with each team member to identify what they have accomplished, what they plan to work on, and any road blocks that might get in the way of their progress. Initiated by the project manager.	Daily	≤10 minutes

Project sponsor update	The project manager discusses the latest project status report with the project sponsor and escalates issues where immediate action is required. Scheduled and led by the project manager.	Monthly	≤1 hour
Project steering committee	Key stakeholders are brought together to receive an update on the project's status and address issues identified by the project sponsor. Scheduled and led by the project sponsor.	Monthly May be less frequent, depending on the phase of the project	≤1 hour
Project advisory	Select stakeholders are brought together to provide the project sponsor with input concerning specific project issues. Scheduled and led by the project sponsor.	Ad hoc	≤1 hour
User group	An open forum for system users, who are briefed regarding the purpose and progress for the IT project. Demonstrations may be provided as an organizational change management tool. Scheduled and led by the project manager.	Ad hoc	≤1 hour
Workshop	Stakeholders are brought together to address a specific need, such as identifying system requirements, developing project objectives, etc. Scheduled by the project manager; led by the team member with the most expertise in the area to be addressed.	Ad hoc	Varies with the stated objective of the workshop
System readiness assessment	Project team members, key members of the organization's IT system management and support staff, and the project sponsor are brought together to make a final determination as to whether the system and the organization are ready for implementation of the solution. The outcome of the meeting is a decision by the project sponsor to move forward with implementation, or not. Scheduled and led by the project manager.	Once, immediately prior to placing the system into production	≤1 hour

Q10 What is configuration management?

Configuration management, as a discipline, includes identifying, tracking, and controlling the latest versions of things purchased for, generated by, and used by the project team. Those things include project artifacts such as plans, specifications, diagrams, manuals, software, hardware, data, and database designs.

Effective configuration management reduces rework associated with team members's imultaneously working from different versions of the designs, software, and hardware.

Consider two software developers who arrive at a meeting with a client to demonstrate a new system they have constructed. When they arrive and attempt to run the demonstration off one of their laptops, they discover that each has been working from a different version of the database. The module developed on the laptop that contains the older database no longer functions as expected. The results are an embarrassing loss of confidence in the team by the project sponsor and stakeholders.

A project's configuration manager can help with this situation. Database versions are logged. Hardware that is acquired for use and its version and configurations are recorded. Software modules are logged in, accumulated, and released as controlled builds. The latest version of the project schedule is recorded and stored in the project's shared files. The information on every one of these items is logged by the configuration manager and made available as a report, usually provided to the project team in the form of a simple spreadsheet that is easily read and used.

Q11 What is change management and why is it important to IT projects?

Change management includes the plans and processes needed to prepare an organization to receive and use a new system. It relies on a deliberate planning process, where organizational needs are assessed and plans are put into place to ensure the change accompanying implementation of a new system is received well by the organization for which the system was produced.

As the saying goes, change is hard. People may not like their current IT system, infrastructure, or manual business process but may have become accustomed to it over the years. As difficult as things might be today, the introduction of a new IT system into the mix changes everything and challenges what comfort they may have derived from their current situation.

Change management seeks to understand the risks associated with implementing a new technological solution within an organization. The process of change management may include information briefings to relieve some of the anxiety associated with the arrival of a potential, new system. It may include involving users in the design and testing of the new system, so that they become invested in that new product and have a stake in its success.

Another aspect of change management involves assessing the organization's infrastructure and identifying what is physically needed to support a new system. It can be embarrassing to implement a new IT system only to find out that the infrastructure available in the organization cannot support it. Change management seeks to identify those support requirements well in advance, plan for them, and build the solution to such challenges into the project.

Project teams are often so focused on the complexities of developing a new system that change management requirements are overlooked. Anticipating what it will take to successfully implement a new system—whether that involves user training, assuaging fears and massaging egos, or making sure the organization's infrastructure can support the new system—can go a long way toward ensuring a successful outcome for any IT project.

Q12 What is a system readiness assessment?

A readiness assessment is a checkpoint review conducted by the project team, for the project sponsor, to determine whether all the pieces are in place for implementing an IT solution. During a readiness assessment, key members of the project team, stakeholders, system users, system support staff, and the project sponsor gather to determine whether the system is ready for use and whether the organization is adequately prepared to receive the new system. Checklists are commonly involved. An example of a readiness checklist used for a recent IT project is provided as Figure 5.3.

FIGURE 5.3 System Readiness Assessment Checklist

No.	Activity	Yes/No/ Not Applicable
1	Has the system been piloted on a smaller scale to lessen impact to the business area in the event problems are experienced?	
2	Have the stakeholders bought off on the implementation and transition plan?	
3	Have maintenance roles and responsibilities for vendors, business staff, and technical staff, been defined and accepted?	

(continues)

(continued)

No.	Activity	Yes/No/ Not Applicable
4	Have future decisions regarding system changes been deferred to maintenance staff unless project team participation is outlined in the maintenance and operations plan or project team assistance is specifically requested?	
5	Have project closeout activities been completed?	
6	Has the security plan or other policies/procedures been put into place outlining remote access security requirements?	
7	Have the requirements of the project's test plan been successfully completed?	
8	Has the project manager walked through the implementation and transition plans with customers and technical support staff and had them indicate their acceptance?	
9	Has additional support staff been made available to support system cutover?	
10	Have all commitments to stakeholders that maintenance staff will be expected to honor been documented and accepted by all parties?	
11	Have outstanding issues, problems, and change requests been clearly documented so the maintenance staff has a clear understanding of the state of the product at the time of turnover?	
12	Has the timing of system turnover been scheduled to minimize the impact on business activities?	
13	Has an electronic mailbox and/or call number been established? Does the plan establish a project mailbox in e-mail where users can centrally report any problems with the new product or system?	
14	Have stakeholders been notified of the implementation date?	
15	Have plans been developed to define exactly how the product or service will be migrated into the business environment, including conversion details, sequencing of events, establishment of the production environment, installation of equipment, etc.?	

16	Has system documentation been completed and made available in final form, either electronically or in hard copy, or both?	
17	Have final system "as-builts" been delivered and made available to the maintenance and support staff, and have they been verified for accuracy?	
18	Has all in-house training been delivered and deemed acceptable by those who will use the new technology?	
19	Has the business and technical staff received their training as close to the implementation of the product as possible (just-in-time training) to ensure that it is current?	
20	Has knowledge transfer been carried out between the vendor and in-house staff?	
21	Is there written production turnover documentation and buyoff from those who will be expected to maintain the new product?	
22	Has a baseline been established for the new technology at the time of turnover, using change management, problem or issue resolution, or other processes to log and track changes to this baseline functionality?	
23	Have maintenance agreements been finalized with outside vendors, if in-house support is not available or capable of maintaining the product?	
24	Have plans been executed to retire and dispose of obsolete or non standard hardware/software, if applicable?	
25	Are there plans for withholding a portion of the vendor final payment until the testing is successfully completed?	
26	Have user licenses been acquired and tracked to ensure that the right number and type are in place?	
27	Has business and project staff agreed that implementation will be complete and transition to maintenance can occur on the planned date?	
28	Are contingency plans in place in case the system/product fails upon cutover?	
29	Are plans in place to implement the new technology/system in parallel with old system/product temporarily so output can be verified between new and old products?	
30	Has the project sponsor given the approval, in writing, for moving ahead with cutover of the new system or technology?	

DELIVERABLES

Q1 What deliverables are developed during the execution process?

The focus of the project execution process is on putting the project's plans into play; getting work done; and producing deliverables in an organized, effective, and cost-efficient manner. The detailed project plans and specifications should be baselined and understood by the project team. The roadmap for constructing and delivering the project's final technical solution should be clearly laid out.

Figure 5.4 provides a list of project deliverables commonly developed during the execution phase of an IT project.

FIGURE 5.4 Execution Phase Deliverables

Deliverable	Description
Deliverable acceptance document	A simple, one-page document on which the team member responsible for reviewing and accepting a project deliverable signs off, indicating that the deliverable is fit for use and accepted as complete.
Deliverables progress summary	An itemized list of project deliverables, cross-referenced to the project's work breakdown structure, that are to be developed during the execution phase, along with planned dates for completion, actual dates of completion, completion status (not started, in-process, complete), and acceptance status.
Detailed test plans	The test management plan is generally developed during the initiation phase of the project. That plan may call out a requirement for a unit test plan, systems test plan, integration test plan, performance test plan, and user acceptance test plan. If those plans were not completed during the initiation phase, it is critical that they be completed during execution and prior to conducting the tests.
Implementation plan	The implementation plan is provided in narrative form and as a schedule or work plan tied to specific activity completion dates and resource requirements for the final effort to deploy a new technical solution. It may include such items as user and maintenance team training, readiness assessment processes, organizational change management activities, and other items that contribute to the successful implementation of the system.

Project status reports	A one- or two-page document that describes the current condition of the project. The project status report may contain a general summary of the project's condition, list of tasks accomplished during the last reporting period, list of tasks to be accomplished during the next reporting period, list of issues that need immediate action, budget status, schedule status, and summary of change control activity.
System readiness assessment report	A brief checklist, signed off by the project sponsor, to indicate that the new system is ready for implementation. A typical readiness assessment checklist designates the following items as complete and ready to support ongoing system operations: production environment readiness, testing and defect remediation, data migration, user and system maintenance and support team training, and system documentation.
Schedule updates	The project schedule is the guiding document for the execution phase of the project. Although the baseline schedule is developed during the planning phase of the project, it is appropriate that updated versions of the schedule be produced at regular intervals during the execution phase. The goal of these updates is to accurately reflect the progress of the project and to make modifications to the schedule as deemed necessary by the project team.
Test results report	Test results should be aggregated during each of the different tests conducted on the system, recorded, and provided for acceptance and signature by the project sponsor once the testing is complete. Test results should identify each test case and its pass/fail status, rework accomplished to remedy defects found during testing, and the outcome of retesting efforts. One set of test results should be provided for each type of testing completed as part of the project plan.
Updated project plans	The project plan should be updated at any point that the need for change is identified. This can, and often does, occur during the project execution phase.
Vendor project status reports	If a vendor has been contracted to play a major role in an IT project, it is essential that the vendor provide a separate project status report. The content of the vendor's report should mimic the content of the project status report completed by the organization's project manager, but the report should be presented from the vendor's perspective, with specific reference to deliverables and activities called out in the contract for its work.

Q2 What comes first—the user manuals, the user acceptance testing, or the training?

There is a logical progression in IT project management that ensures that manuals, testing, and training contain consistent and accurate information and provide the best value to the organization receiving a new IT solution. That progression includes:

1. *Draft the manuals.* User manuals are drafted and provided to the test manager and training manager. The draft user manual forms the basis for training courses developed by the training team, and it is validated against the approved test case inventory identified for user acceptance testing. Discrepancies are resolved in advance of publication of the draft manual to ensure that the test cases in the approved test plan and the content of the user manuals agree, and that training content is consistent with the information provided in the user manuals and what is to be tested on the system.

2. *Train the users.* Members of the test team receive training in anticipation of conducting user acceptance testing, using the draft manuals. The users provide feedback to the training manager regarding inconsistencies between the training and the content of the manual. The manuals and training materials are updated to resolve any consistencies.

3. *Test the system, the training, and the manuals.* The test team completes user acceptance testing. The manuals are validated as a part of the testing, ensuring that the system tested is fully and accurately reflected in the manuals, and that training was sufficient to prepare the test team to engage the new solution with appropriate knowledge and understanding of the system's capabilities and limitations. The manuals and training curriculum are updated to resolve any inconsistencies.

This process, if followed, ensures that once the IT solution is implemented throughout the organization, the training and documentation provided to users and maintenance staff are accurate and of high quality.

DEFECT MANAGEMENT

Q1 What is the best way to manage defects, or bugs, during an IT project?

Defects—often referred to as bugs—arise when some aspect of the system does not function as specified. Defects arise as a result of problems with the system's software, database, hardware, network, communications, business rules, interfaces, and other design elements. Defects commonly come to light during testing, but they can be identified at any point during a project's lifecycle.

Defects should be identified by a test team member, validated by a qualified project team member, and recorded in a defect tracking log. The person responsible for creating the element of the system where the bug was detected should be tasked to analyze the defect, design a solution, and implement the fix. Rework associated with defect resolution must be documented and included in project design documents, user manuals, and other project deliverables as appropriate.

A typical workflow for defect identification and tracking is provided in Figure 5.5.

Q2 What is a defect log and what information does it contain?

Defect logs can be produced manually, in a spreadsheet, or by using sophisticated defect tracking software. An example of a typical defect tracking log is provided as Figure 5.6.

Defects should be prioritized on the basis of their potential impact on a system or its performance. Common criteria for prioritizing defects include the following:

- Priority 1 indicates the system cannot function and the defect must be fixed as soon as possible.
- Priority 2 is an important bug that does not need to be fixed immediately but must be fixed before system release.
- Priority 3 is an optional bug that might or might not be fixed depending on the availability of resources and the schedule.

Defects should be analyzed and reported on a regular basis so that the impact of the potential rework requirements on the project schedule can be identified. The information provided in the defect analysis report (a sample of which is provided as Figure 5.7), for example, provides project management with a clear picture of a project's defect status. In the example, there are six open Priority 1 defects. The average time to resolve Priority 1 defects is 0.5 day; that suggests that three days would be required to resolve all six Priority 1 defects.

Q3 Is it okay to abbreviate testing when the schedule is tight?

The short answer to this question is "No." A new IT solution's quality cannot be ascertained except through testing or actual use. If major defects are uncovered

FIGURE 5.5 Defect Management Workflow

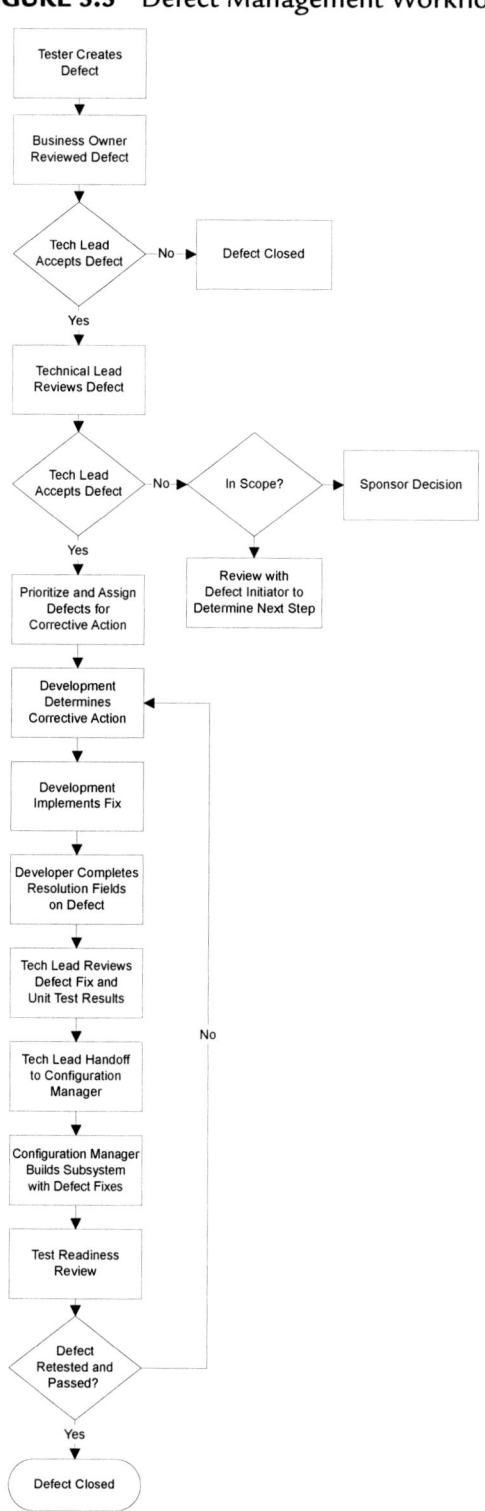

FIGURE 5.6 Defect Log Template

Defect #	Defect Title	Description	Priority	Test Case ID #	Identified By	Date Logged	Assigned To	Date System Change Implemented	Status	Outcome
1	Student enrollment page fields improperly labeled	Change "Kindergarten –Grad 12" to "Kindergarten–Grade 12"	1	3.1	J. Doe	9/9/2012	G. Wiz	10/25/2010	Closed	Fixed
2	Page display is incorrect	-Table headers "Basic Education" and "Categoricals" should be centrally aligned. -Item code M49 is a user input field and should be blank.	2	2.7	B. Smith	9/9/2012	D. Base	Pending	Deferred	Pending

FIGURE 5.7 Defect Analysis

Defect Priority	Total Open	Total Closed	Total Count	Average Time to Resolve
1	6	11	17	0.5 day
2	4	15	19	2.5 days
3	5	2	7	4 days

after the system has been put into production, the business operations of the organization might be negatively impacted. At that point, it is too late to avoid the potential negative impact. Adequate testing ferrets out system defects in advance of the business being burdened by a potentially defective new IT solution.

IT projects are notorious for exceeding schedule and budget. When the schedule is tight and a system needs to be finished in a short period, testing most often suffers. That happens because testing naturally takes place near the end of a project's implementation work plan.

Curtailing testing, no matter the justification for doing so, is not a good idea. It exposes the owners to considerable, unacceptable risk and should be avoided at all costs.

Chapter 6

PROJECT CLOSEOUT

A project closes once the final deliverable solution has been provided to the users and they have accepted the product. It is a time to celebrate and to put the final details in order so the project team can move on to the next project. There can be no greater feeling than completing a successful project. The users have what they need to do their jobs more effectively and efficiently, and the project sponsor's vision is fulfilled.

Some project managers, in their haste to move on to the next project, close the doors on the project office too quickly. They forget the final few tasks that ensure the project is buttoned up, secured, and remembered as the one that succeeded—often against great odds.

PROJECT MANAGEMENT CONSIDERATIONS

Q1 When does project execution end and project closeout begin?

It is handy to conceive of the project management lifecycle as a linear process, with each phase neatly following on the heels of the one before it. For those who work in the field, the linear view of that relationship helps to keep the project management process areas neatly aligned.

Life is seldom as simple as that, and project management is no different. The project closeout process begins whenever artifacts require archiving, although generally with some proximity to final acceptance of the project's deliverable solution.

Although a traditional waterfall approach aligns the project closeout process close on the heels of the project execution phase, experienced IT project managers understand that the two project management processes overlap (Figure 6.1). It is not so important to establish rigid entry and exit criteria for any phase of a project; it is more important to understand the work that needs to be completed in that phase and get it done.

FIGURE 6.1 Project Closeout and Execution Process Linkage

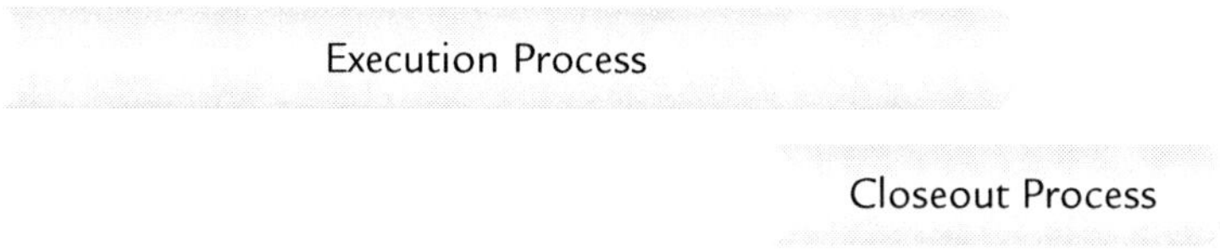

Execution Process

Closeout Process

During the project closeout process, contracts with vendors are completed, the vendor receives its final payments, and the contract documents are signed and filed as completed. As the project team finalizes project documentation, those documents are archived in files stored in perpetuity.

Gathering lessons learned is also an important part of the project closeout process, although lessons learned can in fact be documented during any phase of a project.

Q2 What are the typical activities undertaken during project closeout?

Project closeout includes all the activities needed to shut a project down, whether the project has been successfully delivered or was terminated before its time (Figure 6.2). The goal of project closeout is to tie up contractual and administrative loose ends, prove the project was successfully brought to a conclusion, gather information to make the next project easier, and celebrate the end of the project team's time together as a functioning group.

FIGURE 6.2 Project Closeout Activities Checklist

Checklist Item	Yes	No	NA
Hold a feedback meeting with the client			
• Review commitments that were made			
• Solicit feedback on satisfaction			
• Solicit evaluation of the project process			
Hold team meeting			
• Develop lessons learned			

• Provide/solicit team feedback			
– Team membership			
– Actuals for schedule, staff time, budget			
• Discuss suggestions for project process improvement			
• Celebrate success			
Hold a project review meeting with the project sponsor			
• Review project plan			
• Review project results			
• Identify lessons learned			
• Discuss ideas for improvement, submitted by your team, and ask for client input			

Specific processes that should be defined and executed for project closeout include:

- *Administrative closure procedures*—Releasing project team members, archiving documents, closing project Web sites.
- *Contract closure procedures*—Making final vendor payments, closing out contracts used for the project, completing any administrative actions necessary to report vendor performance.
- *Final products, services, or results*—Validating that the system was provided as intended through an audit of project objectives and requirements and system functionality, completing a project closeout report.
  - *Requirements audit*—An audit of system requirements should be completed using a requirements traceability matrix as its basis. That matrix should list all the requirements approved for the project. The intent of the audit is to validate that each requirement was satisfied by the system that was delivered by the project team. For more information, see the next question in this chapter.
  - *Project closeout report*—Documents the results of a project in a format that is useful to the project sponsor. See the question on project closeout reports later in this chapter.
- *Lessons learned*—A review of the processes and activities used by the project team, validating those that worked out well and identifying opportunities for improvement. This review is commonly carried out as an informal working session with project team members and key stakeholders, brought together one last time before the project is officially adjourned, while the information is fresh

in everyone's minds. Some project managers find it useful to conduct the project's lessons learned session as part of the project close celebration.

Lessons learned documents are brought together in a central repository for access by future project teams working on similar projects. The results of the lessons learned session are provided in tabular form (Figure 6.3) and included as an element of the project closeout report.

FIGURE 6.3 Sample Lessons Learned Record

Area or Topic	Observation and Recommendations
Procurement management (vendor software development process maturity)	Quality Improvement Opportunity When major changes were implemented in the system and tested by the project team, those changes often negatively impacted other areas of the system. This indicated that the vendor did not have adequate control over product configuration during its development process and did not conduct internal quality assurance of its processes and product.
	Recommendations: Require vendors to demonstrate their develop–test, quality assurance, and configuration management processes prior to selection. If those processes are found to be lacking, require their development as a deliverable and tie payment to the successful use of those processes. Require evidence of internal testing and quality assurance by the vendor prior to acceptance of system upgrades and major releases.
Project management (project manager skill)	Validated Practice The project managers and business leads for the project were perceived by senior executives as highly competent leaders and good interpreters of the information technology aspects of the project into language that could be used effectively for decision-making processes.
	Recommendations: Continue to seek out, train, and utilize high-quality personnel in important project management roles.

- *Celebration of the project's success*—A formal or informal gathering of people who have participated in the project to celebrate the project's success, acknowledge the value of their participation, and provide closure. It is important to recognize everyone who was involved in the project, particularly stakeholders who may have taken time away from other important duties to contribute to the project's success. Celebrating a project's success validates the participants' contributions and positions them to more favorably respond the next time a project team asks for their assistance.

Q3 Who leads the project closeout process?

The project manager ensures that the activities associated with project closeout are completed in an effective and timely manner. The project manager is accountable to the project sponsor, is closest to the project, and is the best person to understand exactly what needs to be done to bring a project to a satisfactory conclusion.

Every member of the project team carries some responsibility for documenting lessons learned, generating the content of the project closeout report, and ensuring that the closeout celebration is a great event. Unfortunately, as a project winds down, many of those people move on to the next project before the opportunity arises to participate in project close. Because of that, it is incumbent upon the project manager to gather the information needed for the closeout report as early in the closeout process as possible, debrief departing project team members and stakeholders before they leave the project, identify lessons learned, and find out where to send the departing project team member's invitation for the project closeout celebration.

There is nothing better than sitting back at the end of a project—having successfully submitted a project closeout report—and participating in a project celebration. Invariably, that process stimulates reflective thinking that brings back priceless memories. IT projects are notoriously challenging to deliver, so when you have a chance to bring one to the finish line on budget and on schedule, with a happy project team and happy system users, make sure that you take a moment to reflect and that you provide your team members the same opportunity. You all deserve that moment.

Q4 What is a project archive and why is it important?

A project archive is an organized collection of hard-copy and electronic files maintained by an organization to document all that has occurred on a project. It may be structured as a project Web site using sophisticated automated tools or provided in the form of a steel file cabinet. However it is constructed, the project archive becomes a repository that can be a valuable resource for organizations that carry out IT projects.

Public-sector organizations are required to maintain project archives for a specified period to support formal project audits. In this case, it is critical that all documents, software, and other artifacts be stored in the archive, whether they are in draft or final form. To support public disclosure laws in most states, emails generated by the project team are an auditable project artifact that should be stored in the archive. The emails may not be sanitized, deleted, or altered in any way when they are filed for future review.

Aside from supporting a potential project audit, project archives provide a treasure trove of opportunity for project managers looking for analogous projects upon which to base their own projects' plans. There is no need to reinvent plans and templates when they might be available from a similar project, stored in an organization's archives. Software objects, data models, business architecture, network diagrams, system requirements, and workflow diagrams can all be retrieved from a well-kept project archive and often reused in part or in total.

Maintaining a project archive can be a chore, particularly when the project is moving fast, decisions are being made at a rapid rate, and time is of the essence. To mitigate this situation, project managers often assign a person to act as the project's document manager and archivist. No matter how fast the tempo of the project gets, it remains that person's responsibility to gather and archive project documents. For complex projects, it is not uncommon for a part- or full-time document manager to be hired to ensure the project archive is properly established and maintained.

DELIVERABLES

Q1 How do you document successful completion of an IT project?

A project closeout report provides a great opportunity for documenting the success of an IT project. It articulates the intended outcomes of the project and validates that those outcomes were achieved. If an objective or a set of requirements were not met, those are identified, along with a recommendation regarding how best to deal with those few, remaining open items. Budget, schedule, and human resource utilization are documented for historical purposes.

The topics often addressed in project closeout reports are depicted in Figure 6.4. Such reports are often customized to meet an organization's unique needs.

Q2 How do you confirm that the full scope has been delivered at project closeout?

The most objective way to validate that all of a project's requirements have been met is through a final audit of the project's approved requirements traceability matrix.

FIGURE 6.4 Project Closeout Report Template

Project Closeout Report

Executive Summary
A brief statement that summarizes the major achievements of the project and whether it satisfied the project sponsor's vision and objectives.

Project Background
A short extract of the project background, generally derived from the project charter.

Project Outcomes.
- *Project Successes* – a listing of quantifiable project outcomes, including how well the project performed with regard to budget and schedule limitations, the percentage and/or number of requirements that were satisfied and final statistics that describe how well the system fared during testing and during the pre-production readiness assessment.
- *Project Benefits* – a summary of the objectives that were satisfied by the project, and the specific business value that was provided to the sponsoring organization as a result of those successes.
- *Project Challenges* – unique challenges that were experienced during the project, how they were handled by the project team, and any recommendations for how to address those challenges in the future. This topic may be continued later in the lessons learned section of the report.

Remaining Issues
Identify any open issues raised by stakeholders or project team members which may not have been resolved by the time the project may have been shut down. Note that technical issues should be clearly delineated, documented, and passed on to the application support staff for resolution post-production.

Summary of Lessons Learned
A listing of observations that validates those activities and processes that worked well and those that could have been improved. For areas of improvement, specific recommendations are made for how to implement those improvements.

A requirements traceability matrix (Figure 6.5) provides a detailed list of a system's requirements and documents the alignment of those requirements with design, development and installation, test, training, and project documentation. At the conclusion of a project, the requirements are examined one last time to validate that they have been incorporated into the system as called out in the requirements

FIGURE 6.5 Requirements Traceability Validation Matrix

Specification Section	System Module	Description	Requirement	Trace Areas Confirmed			
				Test Plan	Training Plans	Manuals	Final System
1.6.1	Client Security	Vendor-provided biometric client identification system	Provide visual recognition systems at the point-of-sale location	✓	✓	✓	✓
1.6.1.1	Point-of-Sale Systems	Simple biometrics	Provide fingerprint recognition pads and functionality at the point-of-sale location	✓	✓	✓	✓
1.6.1.2	Point-of-Sale Systems	Provide facial recognition	Provide facial recognition functionality at the point-of-sale location	✓	✓	✓	✓
1.6.1.3	Point-of-Sale Systems	Provide voice recognition	Provide voice recognition functionality at the point-of-sale location	✓	✓	✓	✓

specification document. Project team members create a list of the requirements, walk through the list one requirement at a time, and literally check off each requirement as having been met. If any requirement is found lacking, an appropriate indication of its status and any future plans are appended to the matrix.

When the audit of the requirements traceability matrix has been completed, a report of the audit's findings are presented to the project sponsor for acceptance and inclusion in the project archives. The final requirements matrix is often included as an attachment to the project closeout report.

Chapter 7

PROJECT MONITORING AND CONTROL

Project monitoring and control are carried out by project managers and their teams throughout the life of a project. As soon as resources are committed and money is spent on a project, someone must be held accountable. In the world of IT project management, monitoring and control have a distinct and unique meaning. Do those tasks well, and the project sponsor, team, and stakeholders align with you and support your efforts. Forget these critical responsibilities, and it is nearly impossible to maintain that trust and confidence.

Q1 What tools are used to monitor and control an IT project?

In the world of project management, monitoring and control equate to having the tools in place to help you determine where you should be at any point in time for a project, see where you actually are, and influence the difference. The days of managing high-dollar, high-risk IT projects by the seat of the pants are long past. Today's investors require strict accountability for the high-tech projects they fund.

In a high-speed, accountable world, project managers succeed or fail based on how they lay out their plans and track them through the life of the project. When an IT project slips behind schedule, the project manager is judged not so much by the fact that the schedule has fallen behind as by whether he was able to anticipate that situation, tie the project sponsor into the situation proactively, and come up with a plan to address the situation.

Some of the most effective tools for monitoring projects are the most fundamental to develop:

- *Project schedule*—An accurate project schedule is developed using a spreadsheet or project scheduling program, fully loaded with resources assignments, estimates for each work activity, and actual expenditures kept up-to-date through the life of the project. The information contained in this schedule facilitates the use of techniques like earned value analysis (EVA). The results of an EVA provide objective evidence that a project is on or off schedule, on or off budget, by how much, and how that variance is likely to affect the project's future.

- *Deliverables inventory*—A list of project deliverables can be developed using a simple spreadsheet or word processing document. The list should contain the projected due dates for each deliverable, the deliverable's current status (not started, in-process, or complete), the actual date it was completed, and the name of the person responsible for accepting/approving the deliverable. This list, when combined with the results of the EVA, provides proof that a project is on track or off track in a highly objective manner.

- *Project status report*—This report is provided to the project sponsor and other stakeholders. The content of the report usually addresses the current status of the project, including what has been accomplished during the last reporting period, what tasks are scheduled to be completed during the next reporting period, and any outstanding issues for escalation to the project sponsor for timely resolution. Project status reports may also include major risks confronting the project as well as the status of the project's budget and schedule, stated in objective terms.

- *Issue log*—An issue log identifies questions and concerns raised by stakeholders but not resolved at the time they were raised. Information contained in the log includes the date the issue was identified, its relative priority, a description of the issue, who it was assigned to for resolution, its status (open or closed), and the date it was resolved. This list is essential for ensuring the project manager has a handle on the concerns raised by stakeholders, so those issues do not morph unexpectedly into risks or scope change requests. The old project management axiom is true: Manage project issues or they will manage you. In the latter instance, you will not be perceived as being adequately in control of your project.

- *Risk register*—A risk register identifies the priority risks for the project, their probability of occurrence, the potential impact they might have on the project, a risk management strategy that might prove successful should the risk arise, the name of the person assigned to track the risk, and its current status (open or retired). Risk management is a tool that helps project managers anticipate challenges and opportunities for their projects. If a negative event that was anticipated and listed in the risk register were to occur, the plans developed for managing that risk could be put into place with that much more speed and confidence.

There are as many monitoring and control tools available for project managers to use as there are project managers in the industry. Each person has his or her own style of management. That said, the tools described in this chapter of the handbook are some of the basics that no seasoned IT project manager would be without.

Q2 What is included in an IT project status report and why is it important?

A project status report provides a brief summary of the project's overall condition at any point in time. The goal of a project status report is to communicate important project information to the project sponsor and stakeholders on a regular basis.

As a rule, project status reports are completed and filed by the project manager and addressed to the project sponsor and key stakeholders. In the spirit of full transparency, many project managers feel it wise to make sure their project team members receive a copy of the report as well.

Although the project status report is an excellent communications tool for the project sponsor and the project's stakeholders, it is often the project manager who benefits most from the reporting process. It forces the project manager to remove herself from the details of the project in favor of a higher-level view and see how the project is going as a whole. That can be a healthy perspective, particularly when the small piece that the project manager might personally be working on is going very well but other parts are not doing so well.

The content of the project status report should include, at a minimum, a list of tasks completed during the reporting period, a list of tasks scheduled for completion during the next reporting period, and a list of issues for escalation to the project sponsor. Project status reports may also include key risks confronting the project, a summary of change control activity, and earned value analysis data regarding budget and schedule variances experienced by the project.

Brief project status reports are usually read; those that extend beyond a couple of pages stand the risk of being set aside by project sponsors until they have more time in their day. Two pages or less is recommended for project status reports intended for review by the project sponsor and key stakeholders. In an era of electronic documentation, it is a simple process to produce a brief project status report that contains hyperlinks to files where readers can find more detail if they so choose.

Figure 7.1 provides an example of a simple project status report that has been used for years by successful project managers overseeing IT projects of various sizes.

Q3 How can a project manager manage a technical team when she lacks technical skills?

Admitting what you do not know is the first step toward becoming an effective project manager. It is only one additional small step before you find a way to fill that knowledge gap or find a way around it.

FIGURE 7.1 Project Status Report Template

Client										
Project Name							Date of Report			
Key Performance Indicators										
Overall Project Status		Schedule		Budget		Scope		Risk		Issues
= and Red, Green or Yellow		▲ and Red, Green or Yellow		▼ and Red, Green or Yellow		= and Red, Green or Yellow		▲ and Red, Green or Yellow		▼ and Red, Green or Yellow
= No change from last report ▲ Improved from last report ▼ Downgrade from last report						Green = No Major Issues or Concerns Yellow = Some Concerns Exist Red = Critical Concerns Impact the Project				
Budget at Complete			Planned Value			Actual Value			Earned Value	
Estimate to Complete			Estimate at Complete			Schedule Variance			Cost Variance	
Tasks Completed this Reporting Period										
Tasks Scheduled for Next Reporting Period										
Outstanding Issues								Responsible Team Member		
Issues for Escalation and Immediate Action								Responsible Team Member		

It has been said that any trained project manager can manage any type of project. From a purely theoretical viewpoint, that might seem possible; from a pragmatic perspective, it is simply not true, particularly for IT projects.

Technology has its own language, conventions, and subtleties. This is especially true for IT projects, where the technology behind the discipline changes and evolves at a rate that can be overwhelming. To keep up, an IT project manager has to find a way to either learn each new development or identify those who have that knowledge to fill a potential need on the project. If that project manager is not technically qualified, the latter option holds the most promise.

Successful IT projects thrive under the joint leadership of a business-oriented project manager and a well-rounded technology leader, working as partners as they lead the project team. An experienced technical leader or architect can augment the project manager's capabilities when the project manager lacks those skill sets. Together, they provide the whole package—business and technical—needed to guide an IT project to success.

The question that normally comes up when a project is managed by a project manager and technical lead is, "If they are sharing project leadership, who's in charge?"

This question was addressed in an earlier chapter of this book, but it warrants repeating: Good leaders know when to take charge of the project and when to surrender control to someone else when the situation warrants that action. The de facto project manager can hand leadership off to the technical team lead when the time is right and recapture it when that time has passed.

Q4 What is a code review?

Code reviews are conducted by the senior architect or technical lead assigned to an IT project. Simply stated, that person gathers the project's technical team members together and walks through the software generated by the team, line by line, to ensure it has been developed in accordance with the designs, policies, guidelines, and standards adopted by the project. The goal of the effort is to validate that good code supports the project's approved architecture, policies, guidelines, and standards, and to highlight any remediation that might be required to bring the code into compliance.

For large projects, where a team might generate millions of lines of code, the code to be reviewed is sometimes selected using a random number generator. That tool factors in the total lines of code available for review and uses statistics to randomly select lines of code for inspection. This approach ensures the number of lines reviewed represents a statistically appropriate sampling of the total available code.

Q5 What is an architectural test?

Architectural testing provides a quick and inexpensive method of testing a system's conceptual architecture before it has been finalized. Architectural testing goes beyond peer review and audits of conceptual plans and specifications. Accomplished very early in the design phase of a new system, the approach can provide substantial value at a relatively low cost.

To conduct an architectural test, a portion of the architecture is cobbled together in a very rough approximation of how the system will be organized once it is constructed. A selection of system components involved in the most complex aspects of the architecture is interfaced, and data is pushed through the system to see if the architecture is reasonably functional. Everything developed during the architectural test is intended for the junk heap. No element of the architectural testing is retained beyond the simple validation that the architectural concept is sound and will support the system with a reasonable degree of certainty.

If accomplished in the spirit intended, architectural testing should be brief and inexpensive and should produce tangible results. Detailed design and construction efforts, and the time and money consumed for those purposes, should be saved for later in the project, once the architecture for the system has been confirmed as reasonably sound and system construction is under way.

Q6 What is the best way to manage stakeholder expectations during an IT project?

"Manage stakeholders or they will manage you." Nowhere is that statement more true than with IT projects, particularly in an age when automation is so common and virtually everyone considers himself an expert in technology of some kind.

Project stakeholders include anyone with a vested interest in the outcome of the project. They possess a keen interest in how the project is going yet do not generally function as members of the project team. They may be subject matter experts, future users of the new or improved system, members of the owning organization's senior management team, or people from the general public.

If kept engaged in the project in a reasonable way, stakeholders are valuable sources of information and decision support. If left out of the communications loop on a project, they may inadvertently withhold critical pieces of information needed for the project to be successful. If the situation is dire enough, they may force their way into the project's inner workings until their needs are satisfied, distracting key resources from the project's efforts during times when the project can ill afford to lose those resources.

Stakeholder analysis and management is a discipline accomplished by carrying out the following tasks:

1. Identify the stakeholders by organization and role.
2. Identify each stakeholder's level of interest in, and ability to influence, the project.
3. Identify each stakeholder's specific expectations regarding system requirements, level of involvement, and communication needs.
4. Record each stakeholder's expectations in a stakeholder analysis matrix (Figure 7.2).
5. Assign a team member to manage each stakeholder's expectations.
6. Manage stakeholder expectations and communication requirements as needed, reviewing stakeholder status and management outcomes regularly at project team meetings.

Q7 How much control is too much control over a project team?

An appropriate level of control over IT project team members includes the following:

1. *Assign work early in the project.* Identify work assignments and provide them to the project team members well in advance of the timeframe in which they are to be accomplished. Information that should be included in each work assignment includes a description of the activity, planned start and finish dates, the budgeted hours for the task, the names of those working with the team member, and the criteria for successful completion of the effort.
2. *Delegate management of business and technical resources.* The best person to manage a technical team is one with a good technical background. That person can more readily speak the technical team's language and relate to their efforts than someone who lacks similar skills and experience. The same can be said of the business team, test team, communications team, and so on.
3. *Rely on daily interaction, using a minimalist approach.* Track project team member progress daily, directly or through the team leaders. This should be done with as little distraction from the team members' work effort as possible. One good approach is to hold ten-minute meetings with team member individually to identify the work they have completed, what they plan to do next, and any roadblocks that stand in their way.
4. *Meet collectively over the longer term.* Bring project team members together once each month for an hour-long project update. At that meeting, provide

FIGURE 7.2 Sample Stakeholder Analysis Matrix

Name	Organization	Level of Interest	Potential Impact on the Project	Expectations	Assigned To
J. Smith	Finance and accounting	Very high	Could delay or stop project progress if not satisfied	• Weekly project update • Participate in steering committee meetings • Staff must be included in user activities	Project manager
W. Collins	Contracting	Medium	• Facilitator • Supporter • Can expedite administrative processes	• Kept informed on a monthly basis • Communicated with in advance of administrative need	Project manager
G. Williams	Technical support	High	• Collaborator • Very supportive	• Kept informed on a monthly basis • Incorporated as a subject matter expert during implementation planning and readiness testing	Technical team leader
T. Miller	Software development manager	High	Owns the development resources assigned to the project	• Kept informed on a weekly basis • Desires to know developer requirements 1 month in advance of the need	Project manager
B. Pratt	Chief executive officer	Medium	• Funded the project • Has decision-making authority over all corporate functions	• Kept informed monthly or as needed to resolve project issues.	Project sponsor

team members with an overall status of the project and discuss risks or issues confronting the project. Provide team members with a forum to collectively discuss issues and project challenges and to come to a consensus regarding how to address them.

5. *Hold team members accountable for performance to budget and schedule.* Track project team member expenditures for each piece of work assigned to them by recording their actual hours of work for each task and comparing those to the estimates developed for that task at the beginning of the project. Identify trends and variances, and use that information as a point of departure for discussions about how best to align their efforts in the future.

6. *Practice formal acceptance of deliverables.* Require that someone other than the project team member responsible for developing a deliverable be responsible for reviewing and accepting that deliverable. Review, acceptance, and any rework and retest requirements should be documented to validate acceptance of the deliverable.

Q8 What is earned value analysis?

Earned value analysis (EVA) provides an objective approach for assessing and reporting a project's status. EVA results in metrics that describe a project's status in terms of performance to budget and performance to schedule. It can be calculated manually but is computed easily by using project planning tools such as Microsoft Project.

EVA requires that a detailed project schedule be constructed and loaded with work estimates for each activity or task. It also requires that resources be assigned to each activity, and that those resources be assigned a value such as a cost per hour or a specific material cost.

The analysis part of EVA occurs when the estimated number of hours for each task is compared to the actual number of hours expended by each resource assigned to complete the work. The difference between the two is referred to as a variance. If the number of hours expended is equal to the number of hours estimated to complete a task, and the costs of the resources were consistent with those used when the estimates were made, there would be no cost variance. If more hours were expended to complete the task than estimated, there would be a negative cost variance.

Schedule performance can also be assessed using EVA. In this instance, the goal is to determine whether activities were completed on time as scheduled. For example, consider a task that was estimated as 50 hours of work by a single resource, to be completed during the first month of a project. If, at the end of that month, the work was completed as estimated, there would be no schedule variance. If the task was completed after only 40 hours of effort and the resulting deliverable was deemed complete and acceptable after so short a time, there would be a positive schedule variance.

Some of the basic elements and calculations used to complete an EVA include:

- *Planned value (PV)*—(Also referred to as the budget.) The portion of the approved total cost estimate planned to be spent on an activity during a given period.
- *Actual cost (AC)*—The total of direct and indirect costs expended to complete work on an activity during a given period.
- *Earned value (EV)*—An estimate of the physical work actually completed for a product or deliverable. EV is calculated using the planned costs for the project or activity and the rate at which the team is completing work on the project or activity. EV can be calculated at any point in time during the course of a project, but it must address work that has been validated as being successfully carried out.

A summary of the calculations carried out to complete an earned value analysis includes:

$$\text{Cost variance} = EV - AC$$

$$\text{Schedule variance} = EV - PV$$

The results of an EVA can be used to predict the future with some degree of certainty. Once you have calculated a variance, you can use it to develop indices that can be applied to your current budget estimate and schedule at the completion of the project to determine the potential impact of any trends on the project's eventual cost. That calculation is:

$$\text{Cost performance index: cost variance}/EV$$

$$\text{Schedule performance index: schedule variance}/EV$$

Schedule and performance indices are excellent tools for predicting the future of a project. If an index suggests a 20 percent cost variance at some point during a project, it is a simple task to use that figure to suggest the project might be 20 percent over budget at its conclusion. The same approach can be used to project schedule requirements, given trends in project performance over time.

Be careful when applying EVA early in a project. For a 24-month project, a significant variance during the first two months of the effort does not necessarily provide cause for projecting dire outcomes at the end of the project. During those first two months, the project is being initiated and planned. It is not reasonable to expect performance to budget or schedule to be predictable during so brief a timeframe.

Chapter 8

SCOPE MANAGEMENT

All the money and all the time spent on an IT project are expended for one purpose and one purpose only, and that is to deliver the project's approved scope. Successful projects detail that scope. Effective project managers keep the project's scope firmly engraved in their memories. It is their focus and what they work toward. When projects provide the users of their solutions with the full scope of the users' requirements, the projects are successful.

Q1 How do you define the scope of an IT project?

A project's scope statement is a concise summary of what is included in the project. In the strictest sense, scope consists of the project sponsor's vision statement, the approved objectives for the project, the project's requirements list, and any constraints that may be applied upon those by the project sponsor.

A statement of scope also may identify specific exclusions from a project. This happens most often when the desires of a project's stakeholders exceed the money available in the project sponsor's checkbook. Hard decisions are made, with some objectives and requirements being included as in scope and others excluded as out of scope.

Making the distinction between inclusions and exclusions early in a project goes a long way toward setting appropriate expectations with project stakeholders. They might not like receiving the news that their set of requirements has been excluded from a project's scope, but the earlier they get that news, the earlier they can recover from their disappointment.

Scope is not limited to the things you will build or not build for an IT project. An IT project's scope statement may include specific direction from the project sponsor regarding how the project is to be managed or specific guidance about procurement efforts for the project. Common guidance included in a project's scope statement includes the following:

- All resources for the project will be provided internally from within the organization. Outsourcing is out of scope.
- The new system will use the organization's existing infrastructure, without major additions of hardware, and will leverage existing capacities.
- The new system will be deployed on the cloud.
- Funding for the project will not exceed $500,000.

Redundancies may exist between an IT project's scope statement and other planning documents, such as budgets, procurement management plans, and specifications. There is no rule against redundancy when planning an IT project. In fact, it can be useful, particularly because a project's scope statement is often included as an attachment to a project charter or integrated project management plan. Those documents are frequently disassembled and relied upon separately. Redundancy ensures that the scope statement can stand on its own as a guiding document for project team members.

A project's scope belongs to the organization that owns the project. It is owned by the project sponsor, who carries the authority to make binding decisions and authorize funding to pay for project activities. Any change to the project's scope will impact those project activities, so it should be approved only by the project sponsor.

It would be inappropriate for a project manager to have the authority to unilaterally modify a project's scope. Once the project has been completed, the project manager's role in an organization no longer exists. The project manager is not held accountable for such decisions for the long term after the project is done. The project sponsor, on the other hand, has a vested interest in those decisions because they impact how that person's business will be affected by the technical solution provided by the project team.

Q2 How do you manage scope without squelching the project team's initiative?

A project's scope is set by the project sponsor. The project's technical team exists for the sole purpose of delivering that scope as they develop the project's technical solution. The team's creative processes support the design, construction, and implementation of a technological solution that satisfies scope, not the creation of that scope. From that perspective, there should be no conflict between the technical team's desire to express their creativity and the needs of the project sponsor.

Unfortunately, that is not always the case.

Scope creep is a commonly used term for when a project team's efforts result in system work on functionality and capabilities that exceed the approved scope of a project. If two reports are specified for a project and the project produces four reports, the scope of the project has just crept up by a factor of two.

Scope management attempts to protect the project's approved scope from unauthorized expansion or contraction. It does so by placing disincentives between the approved scope of the project and any team member or stakeholder who desires to make a change to the project's scope.

The first disincentive is the change control form (Figure 8.1). If someone sincerely desires to make a change to scope, he is generally willing to fill out a simple change control form. If he is not serious about the change, the form will effectively keep him from consuming the project team's valuable time with an idea that was probably not worth the effort.

The second disincentive is the project sponsor approval process. When a change control form has been completed by a project team member or other stakeholder, it should be approved only by the project sponsor. People will usually think twice before taking a worthless idea to their boss where their credibility and job might be on the line. The same idea that they might be willing to present to the project manager or a team member will not be taken to so high a level for fear of seeming foolish, hence the benefit of the project sponsor's taking personal responsibility for approving scope change requests.

Having an effective scope management plan in place for a project can save the project manager a good deal of time and effort that might have been expended researching, analyzing, and developing ideas that are not worth the effort.

Q3 What is scope optimization and why is it important to an IT project?

Scope optimization refers to delivering the minimal system functionality necessary to provide the value requested by the user.

The concept of scope optimization is one that is pretty easy to digest if you examine a new IT system or infrastructure a year or so after it has been implemented. Imagine asking the users to inventory the system's functionality that they have actually used. Imagine their surprise when they discover they have never used a large percentage of that functionality, particularly after they paid to have it developed into a new system.

Scope optimization seeks to weed out project requirements that result in system functionality users will never touch in advance of designing the new system. Scope optimization can be achieved by adhering to a program of strict accountability for a project's approved vision statement and objectives.

Project objectives are statements that define the business value the organization hopes to derive from a project. Objectives spring directly from the project sponsor's

FIGURE 8.1 Change Control Form Template

Client Name:				
Project Name:			Date of Request:	
Change Request #		Submitter Name		
Reason for Change				
Recommended Change				
Impact to the System in Development				
Cost Impact				
Schedule Impact				
Date Approved or Disapproved (circle one)				
Project Sponsor Signature				

vision statement and are traceable to that vision statement. If an objective cannot be attributed directly to a word, sentence, or concept expressed in the vision statement, it should be considered out of scope. Ensuring that a project's objectives trace directly to the project sponsor's vision statement is the first step toward scope optimization. Erroneous objectives that could drive the project team's efforts off course from the project sponsor's vision are eliminated.

The second step in the scope optimization process is to ensure objectives are attributed to one or more key project stakeholders.

Project objectives are effective if they use a modified form of the SMART approach. There are innumerable definitions of the acronym SMART. For the purposes of IT project scope optimization, SMART can be spelled out in the following manner:

S—*Specific*. The focus of the objective is limited, confined to a very narrowly defined area of the system, such as "The accounts payable module of the system…."

M—*Measureable*. The value identified with the objective must be objective so it can be measured. An example might be, "The accounts payable module will reduce interest paid for delinquent payments by 30%."

A—*Assignable*. Someone in the organization, preferably a key stakeholder, must personally and professionally sponsor the objective. If no one is willing to sponsor an objective, no time or money should be spent addressing it. In this case, a stakeholder has taken responsibility for the objective, as stated in the case: "… the Chief Financial Officer wants an accounts payable module…"

R—*Realistic*. It must be possible to realize the objective, along with the necessary functionality to bring the objective's potential value to reality. Continuing the example provided above, "an accounts payable module from a recognized top-tier accounting software package vendor…."

T—*Time-bound*. The value specified by the objective should be realized within a realistic period of time, such as "within 6 months of system implementation."

Using the SMART approach ensures that each project objective is assignable and owned by at least one major project stakeholder. To reiterate, if no one wants to own an objective, there is no reason to include it in the project. The requirements necessary to satisfy that objective can be excluded as well, further optimizing scope.

Too often, this step of the scope optimization process is omitted by project managers who, if they have an approved vision statement at all, move directly to defining project requirements without the benefit of defining the project's objectives. Requirements are, by definition, what the project team builds to satisfy project objectives. They spring directly from objectives. If a requirement defined for a project cannot be directly attributed to one or more objectives that are assignable to one or more stakeholders, those requirements may well be erroneous and the functionality may well be something system users simply do not need.

Achieve scope optimization by delivering the minimum scope necessary to satisfy the project's objectives and fulfill the project sponsor's vision. Doing more than that results in unnecessary functionality. It is hard enough to deliver successful IT projects without implementing functionality not required by the user.

Q4 What deliverables are identified in a project's scope statement?

Any deliverable produced for a project—whether it is a document, report, plan, design, specification, diagram, database, data warehouse, or set of code—is considered "in scope" and may be listed in the project's scope statement. For practical reasons, to avoid the scope statement's expanding into a document of immense proportions, deliverables are more appropriately listed in the project's integrated project management plan.

Q5 What is a use case and how does it relate to project scope?

Use cases define functional requirements for a system. A use case is a document or set of documents that identify how a user will interact with a system in a step-by-step, chronological order to complete her business. Use cases do not describe how a system is to be constructed; rather, they describe what the system is to do to satisfy a user's needs.

There are as many formats for use cases as there are business analysts who write them. One format that has proven highly effective in the past is shown in Figure 8.2:

Q6 Why is scope creep so common for IT projects?

On a good day, it is difficult to know exactly what to include in an IT project's scope. Much of what is envisioned for an IT project at the beginning of its life cycle is based on a sketchy understanding of the organization's needs. The technology required to satisfy those needs may never have existed before in the organization. It is a rare business or agency that can describe a project's scope on day one of the project and get it exactly right. For the rest, once construction starts on a new system or infrastructure, reality sets in and the project's scope tends to move around a bit.

Changes occur as projects progress. Knowledge is gained. Stakeholders previously unknown arrive on the doorstep of the project office and suggest additions and deletions to scope that add to the value the organization might realize from the project.

From within the project team, once the first units of code are developed, tasks deemed possible at the beginning of the project become less so. Constraints are revealed as the team works through the process of progressive elaboration and designs are fleshed out. The limitations of the team's experience and their understanding of the technology become apparent and adjustments are made. When those changes result in modifications to the project's approved scope, scope creep ensues.

FIGURE 8.2 Use Case Template

Project Name:		Date:	
Use Case Name:			
Use Case Identification Number:			
1. Description of the Use Case:			
A brief narrative that identifies the business function addressed by the use case and the goal or value to be realized by the use case.			
2. Actors:			
The actors – those persons or other systems – who play a role in the use case are identified			
3. Business Process Flow			
3.a. Normal Processes:			
Defines the normal business process, step by step, that is carried out to complete the use case the majority of the time by actors			
3.b. Exceptional/Alternative Processes:			
Defines, step by step, the flow of the business process that is followed under exceptional circumstances.			
4. Workflow			
This section may include or reference any related workflow diagrams that support the business case.			

Scope creep is insidious and often sneaks up on a project team at the worst possible time. It might arrive as a minor adjustment to a requirement or a shortcut for providing some aspect of desirable functionality. When this process is not controlled, the final product delivered to the customer might look nothing like what was intended. It's the classic case of the fisherman who wants a row boat. By the time the salesperson, the production people at the manufacturing plant, and the research and development people get done with his request, he receives a 40-foot yacht. The fisherman might even think the yacht is a good idea—until he tries to launch it into the river where he fishes and it simply won't fit.

IT projects are notoriously difficult on budget and on schedule. Scope creep, if allowed to occur, only exacerbates the situation. A better solution is to make sure the project team is intimately familiar with the project's approved scope and that solid change control processes are in place and enforced to preclude its occurrence.

Q7 What causes late-stage change requests that cost so much and slow projects down?

There is nothing more frustrating than nearing the end of a challenging IT project and having a major change request dropped on your desk. If the change is significant enough, it can bring the project to a halt. At the least, it will cost the project precious time and money as it is assessed and implemented before moving the project's solution into production.

Late-stage scope change requests typically arise from one source: overlooked and neglected stakeholders. The stimulus for the change request is often related to an issue identified by a stakeholder early in a project that was not adequately addressed at the time it was raised. Those early issues are often related to stakeholder expectations and specific project objectives or requirements. If the issue was not addressed adequately when it was raised, critical information regarding those objectives and requirements may have been overlooked. The stakeholder inevitably shows up later with a disappointed look on her face and a demand that the issue be addressed now, when significant redesign and rework might be required.

Other stakeholders might have been totally overlooked during the early phases of a project. In that case, their input was neither requested nor received, and key project objectives and requirements were inadvertently omitted from consideration. Stakeholders also tend to show up at the least opportune time and demand that their critical piece of functionality be implemented in the system, causing delays to the project and added expense for the project sponsor.

These examples occur all too often. The only solution is to exercise good stakeholder management as an integral part of the project management process. Whether the stakeholder is a potential system user, someone who is paying for the project, or a person closely associated with the project, it is good to pay attention to his needs. A good way to avoid late-stage change requests and the impact they can have on the project is to communicate with those stakeholders early in the project and often throughout the project.

Q8 Who should approve change requests for an IT project?

Only one person or group of people on a project own the project's scope: the project sponsor(s). That person has control over the money that pays for the project's resources. Any change to a project's scope affects the cost of the project. Increase project scope, and the project will cost more. From that standpoint, the project sponsor—the person who holds the project's checkbook—is the only person who should approve scope changes.

From a more practical standpoint, designating the project sponsor as the only approval authority for change requests has many benefits. People think twice before suggesting a change to a system if they must justify that change to their employer. Having the project sponsor approve change requests relieves the project manager from the burden of considering each stakeholder's new idea for the project and allows her to focus her time more appropriately on planning the project and managing the day-to-day activities of the project team.

Chapter 9

TIME MANAGEMENT

There never seems to be enough time to do an IT project. The IT project manager's greatest worry often seems to be the project's schedule, as if there are not enough things to fret about already.

Laying out a well-thought-out and realistic schedule for a project can be a challenge for any project manager. Identifying all the tasks required to construct a new system, modify an existing system, or install infrastructure upgrades is a complex task. Estimating the duration of those tasks, laying them out in a logical order, and assigning resources to each task require discipline and rigor. About the time the team completes that complicated effort, the boss shows up with a new schedule constraint. Now the team has 12 months to complete the project rather than the 16 they had planned on.

The discipline of time management is a key skill set project managers and their teams must master. In a fast-paced world, opportunities are presented and extinguished at a rapid rate. Having the right solution in place to leverage those opportunities when the time is right can make the difference between occupational survival and disappointment.

But time management goes beyond constructing a good schedule. It includes planning the use of resources and ensuring expectations are realistically set when planning out a project team's day, week, month, and entire project. A good schedule speaks to stakeholders and their need for confidence that a team can work together well to produce a quality technical solution, given the time available for the project.

Time management deals with one of a project manager's greatest resources and most bothersome constraints. Master it and your project's chances for success increase exponentially.

Q1 What is the best way to develop a schedule for an IT project?

Ask any writer and he will tell you that every story has been written; it is only the characters and settings that change from author to author. The same is true for IT projects: Every IT project has already been done. The business environment, the project team members, and how the technology is applied might change, but otherwise, IT projects generally run to type, pretty much like stories. The good news from this analogy is that you do not have to build your project's schedule totally from scratch. There is another project out there, much like yours, that you can use as a model.

Good IT projects rely on a fixed set of constants as their starting points:

- *Project initiation*, including initial discovery and chartering of the project by the project sponsor
- *Project planning*, including work plan and schedule development
- *Project execution*, including system design, software acquisition and/or development, testing, training, readiness assessment, and final system acceptance
- *Project closeout*, including validating that project requirements and objectives have been met, gathering lessons learned, crafting the project closeout report, archiving files, and having the project closeout celebration.

Given those starting points, the first, brief attempt at creating a project schedule would look like Figure 9.1.

Once the project sponsor's vision statement, project objectives, and requirements are in place, you have what you need to begin adding the balance of the project's detail. Identify the requirements the team needs to build to satisfy the project's objectives, and the draft project schedule begins to take shape (Figure 9.2).

For the next step of the process, identify the tasks that must be completed to satisfy the project's requirements. Organize those tasks in a logical order, estimate the work required to complete the tasks, and the schedule takes on a level of detail that promises a successful effort.

The sample detailed schedule provided in Figure 9.3 was taken from an actual project. It presents a small fraction of the information contained in the full work plan, but it illustrates the level of detail of a quality project schedule.

The final step includes assigning resources to each task identified in the project schedule. Resource constraints, such as four-day workweeks, planned time off, and schedule conflicts that might arise, must be recognized. This final level of detail puts the finishing touches on the project's schedule and provides a realistic picture of what it takes to complete the project.

The first, best effort at producing a project schedule should be free of time constraints imposed by the project sponsor or any other stakeholder. It is essential that the project team develop a realistic picture of what it takes to deliver the full scope of the project without bias that might taint the estimates provided by the project team.

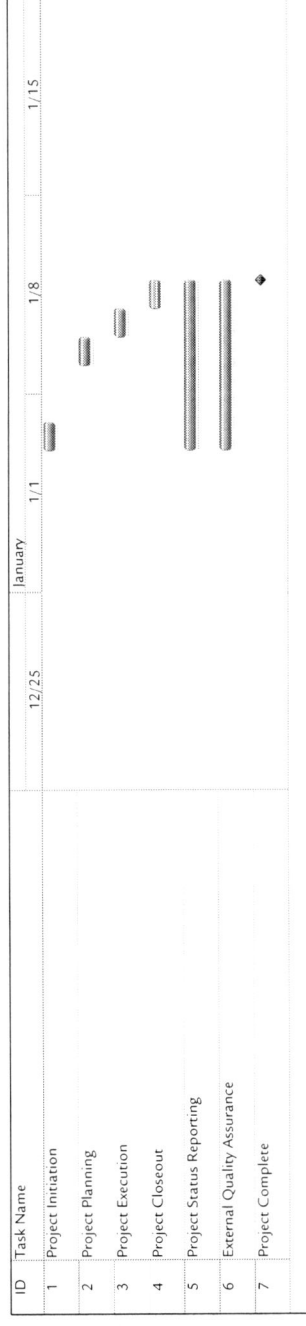

FIGURE 9.1 Project Schedule Development: Step 1

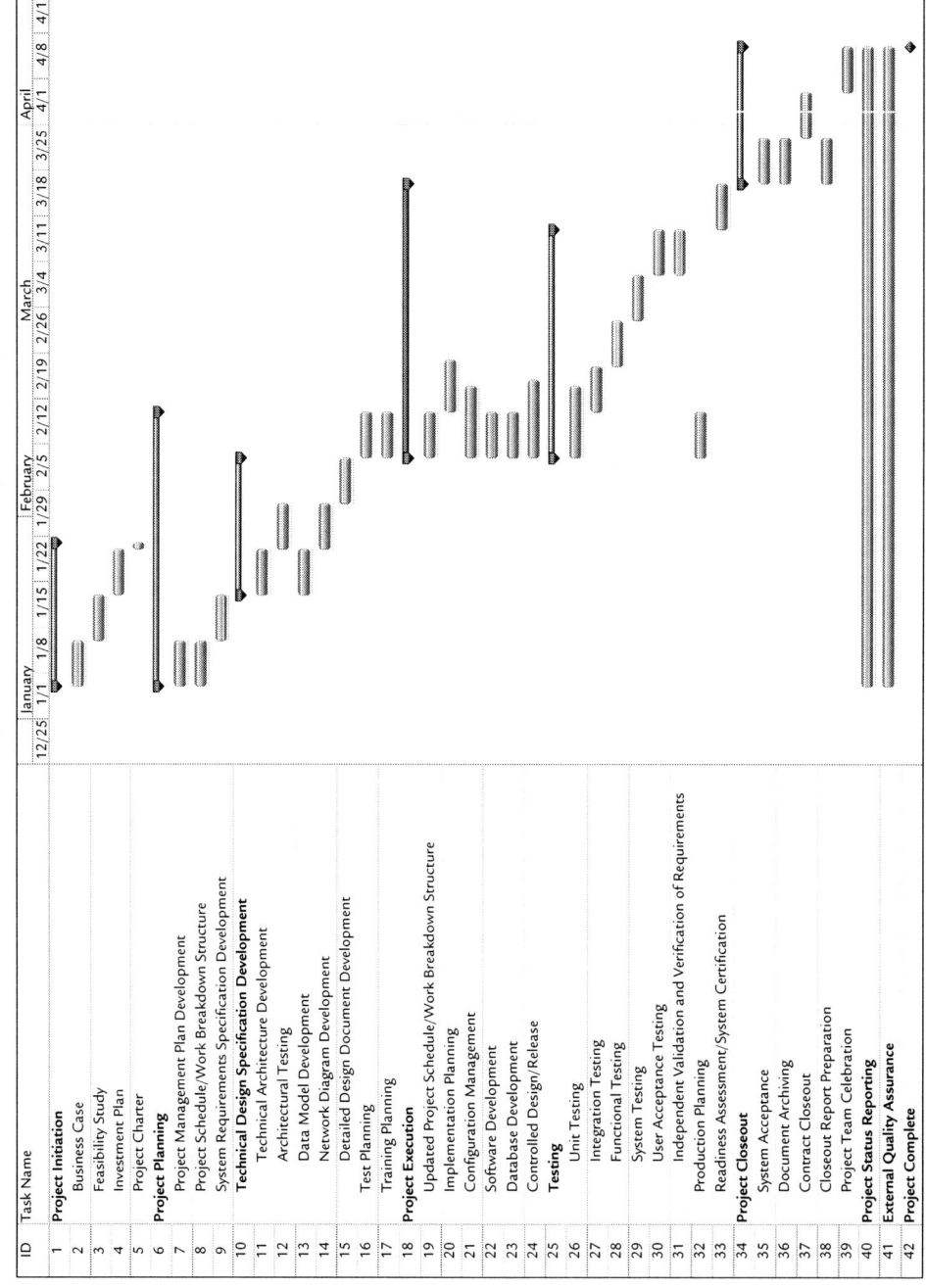

FIGURE 9.2 Project Schedule Development: Step 2

Chapter 9 ■ Time Management 143

FIGURE 9.3 Excerpt from a Detailed Project Schedule

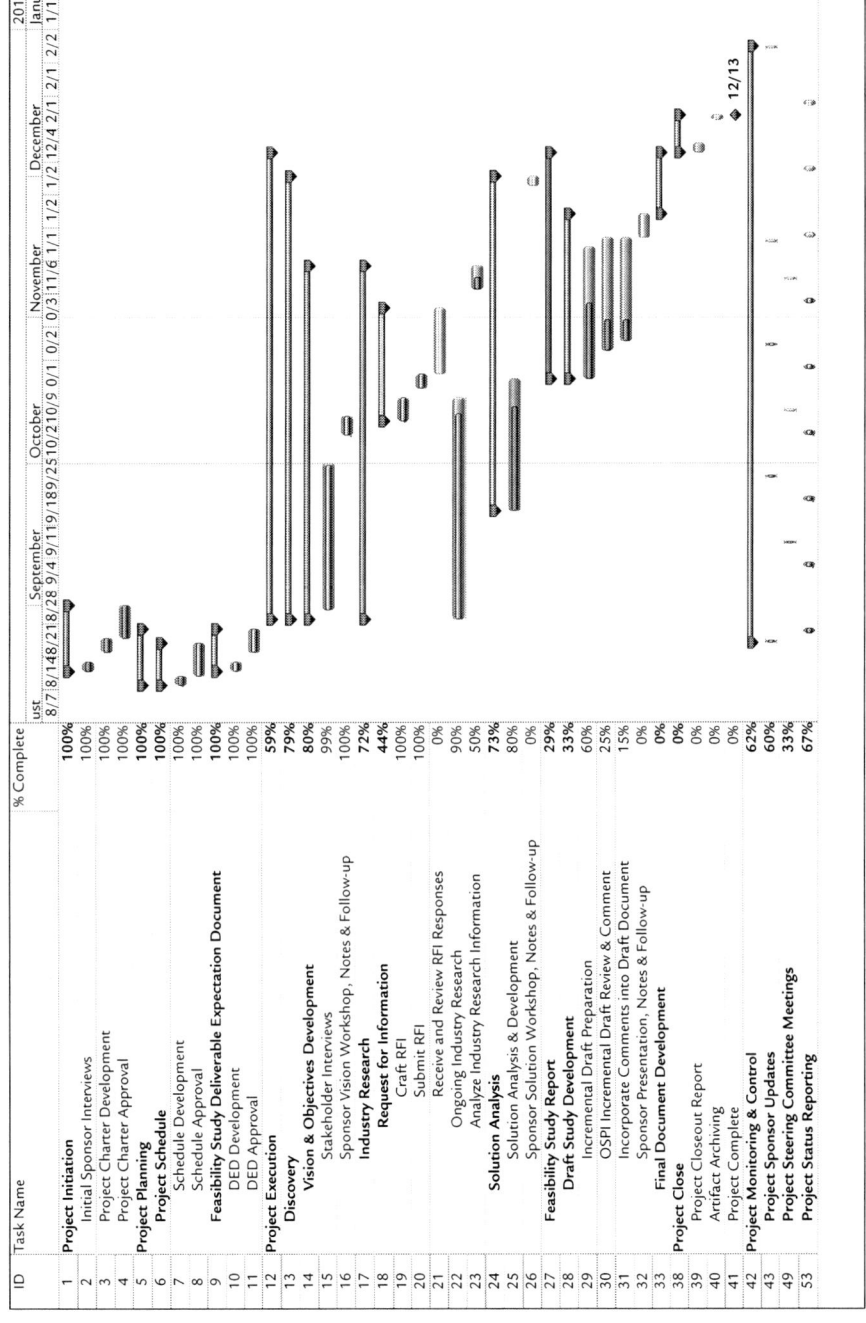

Once that naïve schedule has been developed and baselined, the project manager and the project team can compare it against any constraints established for the project to determine the impact of those constraints from a position of knowledge. If the naïve schedule suggests a completion period of 12 months for a project and the time constraint imposed by the project sponsor is ten months, the project team is better positioned to address any changes to the project's scope that might be necessary to support the shorter schedule or to justify the need for the additional two months.

Q2 How do project schedules differ based on the type of IT project?

Four of the most common types of IT projects are those where a solution is to be custom-built, those where a preconfigured solution is purchased off the shelf, those where a combination of the first two options is used, and infrastructure projects.

The process of developing project schedules remains the same regardless of the type of project. Follow the basic steps described earlier in this chapter, and your project should start out on solid footing. What differences there might be are minimal. Figure 9.4 provides a side-by-side comparison of the differences between some of the various types of IT projects and common elements of IT project schedules. Note that the differences are minimal in terms of breadth of activity.

FIGURE 9.4 Comparison of Activities by Project Type

	Type of Project			
Project Activities	Custom Software Development	Software Package Implementation	Software Integration	Infrastructure
Ongoing project management	X	X	X	X
Project Initiation				
Project management environment setup	X	X	X	X
Document project scope	X	X	X	X
Identify project risks	X	X	X	X

Identify initial project issues to be resolved	X	X	X	X
Develop project charter	X	X	X	X
Project Planning				
Integrated project management plan development	X	X	X	X
Project schedule development	X	X	X	X
Identify tasks	X	X	X	X
Estimate task duration	X	X	X	X
Assign resources	X	X	X	X
Draft project schedule	X	X	X	X
Review schedule with project team	X	X	X	X
Define and document requirements	X	X	X	X
Define technical requirements	X	X	X	X
Develop high-level architecture	X	X	X	X
Generate high-level design	X	X	X	X
Develop detailed design	X	X	X	X
Peer review of detailed design	X	X	X	X
User collaboration and comment	X	X	X	X
Project Execution				
Application development	X		X	

(continues)

(continued)

Project Activities	Type of Project			
	Custom Software Development	Software Package Implementation	Software Integration	Infrastructure
Development team kickoff meeting	X	X	X	X
Environment preparation	X	X	X	X
Architecture review and system acquisition if necessary	X	X	X	X
Set up physical environment	X	X	X	X
Set up development environment	X	X	X	
Set up test environment	X	X	X	X
Base architecture code development	X		X	
Document specifications for storage and access control	X	X	X	
Assess capacity requirements, current and future	X	X	X	X
Draft test plan	X	X	X	X
Database development	X		X	
Solution construction	X	X	X	X
Develop custom features	X	X	X	X
Code development	X		X	
Prepare test scripts	X	X	X	X
Unit test and rework	X	X	X	

Develop standard features		X	X	
Configure standard features		X	X	
Test standard features and rework		X	X	
Test interaction with database	X	X	X	
Freeze development	X	X	X	
Controlled software build	X		X	
Integrated system test	X	X	X	X
Data migration planning	X	X	X	
Migrate data	X	X	X	
Test plan development	X	X	X	X
Develop training strategy and materials	X	X	X	X
Conduct training	X	X	X	X
Assess deployment requirements	X	X	X	X
Assess production environment	X	X	X	X
Configure live environment	X	X	X	X
Software installation	X	X	X	
Initial integration testing	X	X	X	X
System and performance testing	X	X	X	X
User acceptance testing	X	X	X	X
Final integrated system acceptance	X	X	X	X

(continues)

(continued)

Project Activities	Type of Project			
	Custom Software Development	Software Package Implementation	Software Integration	Infrastructure
Final deliverables	X	X	X	X
Plan for support and maintenance	X	X	X	X
Project Closeout				
Project closeout report	X	X	X	X
Validate requirements delivery	X	X	X	X
Archive files	X	X	X	X
Conduct project close celebration	X	X	X	X

Q3 How does requirements traceability factor into development of a project schedule?

Requirements traceability provides the backbone of the IT project schedule.

By way of review, requirements traceability starts with the project sponsor's vision, which clarifies the project sponsor's expectations regarding what the project's solution will look like, how things will change once the solution is delivered, who will be affected by the solution, and the value the project will provide to the organization. Project objectives are statements of the value the owning organization expects to receive from the IT project, and they trace directly to specific elements of the project sponsor's vision statement. Requirements are the things the project team builds to satisfy the project's objectives. Every requirement must trace to one or more objectives and must be defined to the level where the project team understands and can estimate the work, or tasks, that must be done to build that requirement.

The objectives, requirements, and tasks identified for the project form the basis for all plans and specifications developed during the project's planning process. They are the substance of the project's execution process. They are what is validated during the project closeout process. The requirements traceability process provides the means for the project team to define and construct a schedule that is tightly focused on the project sponsor's vision.

Q4 Who manages an IT project's schedule?

The project manager is accountable for the project schedule. A professional project scheduler might be assigned to the project (and in fact there is now a credential for such individuals), but the schedule remains under the direct ownership of the project manager.

The project schedule details a project's effort across time. It sets expectations for the project team and stakeholders, and it provides a valuable communications tool for the project manager. It serves as the basis for ongoing project status reporting and enables the project manager to maintain control over the project's efforts. From those standpoints, it is incumbent upon the project manager to ensure the project schedule is well constructed and maintained through the life of a project.

Q5 What common risks are associated with IT project scheduling?

Figure 9.5 shows the general types of risks and risk management strategies related to project schedules that IT projects commonly encounter.

FIGURE 9.5 Common IT Project Risks

Potential Risk	Risk Management Strategy
Senior Management Involvement Inadequate top management, sponsorship, and support results in decision-making and issue resolution that are not timely, causing the project's schedule to extend over time.	*Avoid the risk.* • Ensure the appointment of a qualified, committed project sponsor before the project begins. • Commit to a clearly articulated, written vision statement for the project, signed by top management.
Stakeholder Commitment Lack of internal and external stakeholder commitment results in resources not being available as needed to participate in the project, causing the schedule to slip over time.	*Avoid the risk.* • Establish a steering committee consisting of diverse leadership from stakeholder groups. • Engage that committee in the scoping effort for the project.

(continues)

(continued)

Potential Risk	Risk Management Strategy
Expectation Management Stakeholder expectations do not match project vision, goals, and objectives. The resulting conflict detracts from project progress and causes increased schedule and cost requirements.	*Mitigate the risk.* • Develop a deliberate project communications plan that clearly identifies key project stakeholders and identifies requirements for communicating with those stakeholders in a meaningful and direct manner. • Ensure full transparency is incorporated within the project's structure to instill stakeholder trust and confidence.
Project Team Experience Limited large-scale project experience within the project team detracts from the team's ability to deliver the project on time and within budget.	*Mitigate the risk.* Establish a firm set of qualifications for key project staff and adhere to them as standards for appointment to the project. *Transfer the risk.* Hire qualified consultants and contractors to augment the project team as necessary. Ensure they are covered by an appropriate level of errors and omissions, and personal liability insurance.
Change Management Processes Inadequate change management processes needed to prepare the organization(s) to implement the new program cause users to hesitate to accept the new solution, extending the schedule and resulting in additional project costs.	*Avoid the risk.* Develop a comprehensive implementation and communications plan to ensure stakeholders are prepared for the program before its implementation
Inadequate Testing Inadequate testing process for automated systems results in the solution's not being adequately tested, with potential user rejection. This stimulates the need for rework with implications for project schedule and cost.	*Avoid the risk.* Ensure that test plans are clearly documented and approved well in advance of program testing.

Resource Availability Internal or external competition within the participating organizations for resources critical to the project results in schedule delays and the need to hire outside resources to augment the team.	*Mitigate the risk.* Gain the commitment of top management early in the project and formally designate the project as a priority for the organization. *Avoid the risk.* Contract for outside resources as necessary to accommodate resource nonavailability.
Scope Management Lack of adequate scope management processes to ensure the project's original vision and objectives are preserved results in scope creep with implications for project cost and schedule.	*Mitigate the risk.* Document project scope management processes and adhere to them. Ensure changes to scope, schedule, and cost are approved only by the project sponsor.
Schedule Constraints Constrained project delivery timelines result in a decreased ability to deliver the approved project scope.	*Mitigate the risk.* Ensure project timelines are initially developed without time constraints. Apply realistic constraints to the initial project timeline, note the resulting risks for the project, and manage those risks accordingly.
Project Planning Resource Constraints Key resources are not available for development of the work breakdown structure and near-term project activities due to conflicting duties, competing projects, and normal work duties. This results in delays in the project schedule.	*Mitigate the risk.* Develop detailed work plans that project resource requirements early and update them on an ongoing basis. Publish resource requirements early in the project to allow resources to plan for their involvement.
Key Resource Departure The departure of key resources during the project threatens the ability to move the project forward within the approved schedule.	*Mitigate the risk.* Identify backup resources to support potential losses as they are identified, and train or hire as necessary to fill the potential gaps in project team skill sets.

(continues)

(continued)

Potential Risk	Risk Management Strategy
Project Complexity The project is revealed to be substantially more complex than originally defined by the users, creating late-stage requirements for redesign and rework and impacting project schedule and cost.	*Mitigate the risk.* • Implement a program of constant user involvement so that progressive elaboration of the system's scope occurs over time, with constant user input, rather than late in the project when the cost of change is substantially greater. • Implement a scope management plan that requires all potential changes to project scope to be reviewed and approved by the project sponsor to ensure changes are kept to the minimum necessary to meet the users' needs.

Chapter 10

COST MANAGEMENT

Project cost management presents the IT project manager with a significant and highly effective tool for managing project performance. When a project's activities are estimated, budgets can be constructed. Actual costs for the project can then be compared to the estimates to determine whether things are going according to plan. If actual expenditures exceed estimates, a cost variance occurs.

Cost variances are indicators that there is a need to dig into the situation and determine the cause of the difference between the estimated cost of work performed and the actual cost of work. Sometimes a variance suggests work that was done beyond the approved scope of the project; other times, it means a task was more complex than originally thought. In every case, it provides good information that a project manager and project team can use to assess the status of the project and make appropriate adjustments to project plans and stakeholder expectations.

Q1 Why is cost management so difficult for IT projects?

Cost management is an essential task within the project management discipline. All too often, project teams exhaust their budgets while diligently trying to satisfy customer needs, never knowing how much of their budget remains to complete the project. They run out of money before the project is done. An opportunity is lost, stakeholders are disappointed, and careers are jeopardized. Most of these potential problems can be managed through effective project cost management.

Many of the challenges associated with project cost management stem from the failure of project management to implement a fully loaded project schedule that contains sufficient resource cost and work estimate information to provide value to the project. When the project team expends effort against the project's schedule, that effort cannot be easily converted into accurate cost information, and control over project costs becomes questionable.

Organizations with payroll systems that attribute employee costs to specific projects are, sadly, all too rare. This places a significant burden on the IT project manager when it comes to tracking project costs. IT projects occur infrequently for most businesses, and the need to track such costs is commonly overlooked. As a result, project managers impose time-tracking requirements on their teams, in addition to the requirements imposed by the organization for payroll purposes. When the project team enters an intense phase of the project, this redundant timekeeping requirement gets lost in the work, and control over project costs weakens.

There is no easy way to track project costs. The single best approach is through diligence and attention to detail on the part of the IT project manager. Construct a fully loaded project schedule, which includes realistic estimates, resources assigned to each task, and costs attributed to each resource, and effective project cost management is greatly facilitated.

Capture actual hours of effort by project team members and costs for materials, compare those to project estimates, and project cost management can be maintained with ease and accuracy. Add the support of an organization's accounting department, and the project manager has a complete set of cost management tools that ensure project costs are well identified, tracked, and controlled.

Q2 What costs are typically associated with an IT project?

Some of the more common costs tracked for IT projects include:

- *Salaries and wages*—These costs are associated with employees of the organization that owns the project and are commonly associated with an hourly wage or equivalent. They do not include payments made to contractors or vendors that are not paid directly or indirectly by the organization.

- *Employee benefits*—These costs are tracked as payments made for employee benefits that extend beyond the basic hourly wage. Costs for benefits may include payments to retirement plans, unemployment insurance, medical insurance, and so on. Many projects omit these costs due to the difficulty in identifying them and separating them from salaries and wages. As an alternative approach, many projects track "fully loaded" salaries and wages, which include benefits. As long as the approach is consistently applied throughout the project, the accuracy of the data should be acceptable.

- *Personal service contracts*—These costs are commonly associated with consultant contracts and other procurements that acquire expert services, rather than the purchase of things.

- *Communications*—These costs are associated with keeping project team members, stakeholders, and others informed of key elements of project information. They may include the costs of advertising, technology, subscriptions, and so on.

- *Hardware rent/lease*—These are the costs attributed to the nonpermanent acquisition of hardware. They are realized as daily, weekly, or monthly and are incurred for a finite period.
- *Hardware maintenance*—These costs are associated with the ongoing upkeep of hardware used to develop the deliverable solution as well as hardware on which the solution will be hosted.
- *Software rent/lease*—These are costs attributed to the nonpermanent acquisition of software. They are realized as daily, weekly, or monthly and are incurred for a finite period.
- *Software maintenance and upgrade*—Most commonly associated with software package deployment and integration projects, these costs are related to keeping that software up to date on projects that might extend over a long period. These costs may include direct costs from the software vendor as well as project team costs for loading and managing the software upgrades and carrying out routine software maintenance.
- *Travel*—Travel costs, ranging from the costs associated with flying in a subject matter expert to those for traveling to vendor sites and reviewing the efforts of team members distributed across the globe, can occur on any project. If the travel is related to the project, its cost should be captured and reported.
- *Overhead*—These costs are related to the buildings, offices, equipment, and utilities that might be used to support a project. Many organizations do not associate these costs with projects because the project team might be borrowed resources and work from the same office space that they occupy to carry out their other duties. If office space is dedicated to the project team, however, identifying, recording, and reporting these costs might be appropriate.
- *Other costs*—If money is expended to support a project, those costs should be recorded and attributed to that project. This becomes very important once the project has been completed and the organization computes a return on investment (ROI) for the project, i.e., how much value the project provided in light of how much was spent to implement the new system or infrastructure. If the costs recorded for the project are not inclusive and accurate, the ROI calculated might not be valid.

Q3 Who is responsible for tracking project costs for an IT project?

It is the project manager's responsibility to track project costs for an IT project. Some organizations provide accounting or bookkeeping resources to project teams. Those persons facilitate the cost management processes and ease much of the burden for the project manager, but the project manager remains responsible and accountable for interpreting the information provided by those members of the project team.

Q4 What information is contained in an IT project's budget/cost management plan?

Effective project managers develop budget management plans that provide the tools to ensure financial expectations are set and project costs are contained and tracked. A checklist for that planning process is provided as Figure 10.1.

FIGURE 10.1 Budget Planning Checklist

Budget Planning Area	Yes	No	NA
1. Financial controls			
2. Baseline project budget			
a. Project budget summary			
b. Requirements and processes for release of funds to the project			
3. Roles and responsibilities for the financial management control processes			
a. Check and balance system that separates authority for expenditure reporting from authority to purchase/encumber project funds			
b. Clear delegation of authority to purchase/encumber project funds			
4. Integration with existing accounting and budget procedures			
5. Financial status reporting			
a. Identifies acceptable and unacceptable budget variances and the process for reviewing, reporting, and responding to them			
b. Project-specific financial tracking tools and controls			
6. References to important fiscal documentation			
a. Budget decision packages			
b. Decision papers			
c. Feasibility studies			

d. Staff studies			
e. Fiscal notes			
7. Contracts and contract management			
a. Milestone acceptance criteria for payments to contractors, if applicable			
b. Acceptance criteria and payment milestones have been developed for contractors			
8. Identifies financial records that will be maintained for the project			
9. Also consider			
a. Financial subject matter experts, from the sponsor's organization, who will assist			
b. Mechanisms for cross-project financial planning/reporting and other nonstandard financial organizations and calendars, such as those associated with federal grants			
c. Project-specific chart of accounts to facilitate maintenance of financial records			
10. Has the budget been reviewed by the project team and all internal and external stakeholders?			
11. Have the stakeholders agreed to the control and reporting procedures?			
12. Is integration with the change management plan to be continually assessed?			
13. Are financial reports to be provided for status reporting?			

Q5 What risks are commonly associated with cost management for IT projects?

Project risks commonly associated with IT project cost management include:

- *The cost of technology*—Technology develops at an ever-increasing rate. One day, a new technology is priceless and acquisition estimates reflect that situation. The next day, what was new becomes commonplace and cost estimates developed before no longer apply. Previously existing software platforms move out of production, and replacement technology must be acquired. The relative instability of the technology industry makes IT project cost management a definite challenge for any project manager or team.

- *Access to trained technologists*—As technology changes and advances within the industry, access to resources with the skills necessary to work with that technology becomes challenging. Those who are available require premium salaries and might be scarce. For projects covering multiple years, even those resources' skill sets can become obsolete, requiring the project team to rethink its resource requirements and expend additional budget training existing project team members.
- *The absence of accurate cost-tracking tools*—If cost accounting is not automated, the data associated with tracking project costs will be subject to the inaccuracies and errors commonly associated with manual management of information.
- *Project team complacence*—The culture of a project team is set by the project sponsor and project manager. If those two individuals consider cost management a priority for a project, project team members will respond accordingly. If that zeal for accurately tracking project costs is not encouraged from senior project management, project team members will focus their efforts on other tasks they deem more important.
- *Organizational orientation*—The organization that owns a project sets the policies and procedures for routine tasks such as cost accounting and management. If the topic of cost management is not viewed as a critical element of the project team's methodology, the project will reflect that perspective and make cost control that much more difficult to maintain.

Q6 What is the best way to manage contract resources on an IT project?

Contract resources should be incorporated into project budgets and cost management tools in the same manner as resources acquired from within the organization. They should be associated with specific project tasks and their costs tracked against those tasks. If a consultant is hired on an hourly, daily, or fixed-cost basis, the cost of the consultant's effort should be incorporated into the project budget accordingly.

Chapter 11

QUALITY MANAGEMENT

Ask any project sponsor for an IT project what he wants out of his project, and he will usually come up with the same response—a quality product. He might not understand exactly what that means when it comes to IT projects, products, and systems, but he knows he wants it.

Quality is easier to achieve than it might seem on the surface. It has been a topic of conversation and corporate interest for decades, and there is a reason for that. Quality IT solutions satisfy system users. A lack of IT solution quality impacts business functions and threatens an organization's livelihood. The solution for any IT project manager is to plan quality into her projects early on and ensure that her project team's focus is on delivering a quality project.

Q1 What is quality and how do you plan for it?

In the IT project management world, quality means satisfying specifications within cost and schedule constraints. It is an aspect of the triple constraint (Figure 11.1), which suggests that a project's scope, schedule, and cost are bound together and represent the user's needs and expectations. Satisfy those expectations, and you will achieve a quality outcome.

From a software engineering perspective, quality is achieved when the requirements identified by the system users have been incorporated into the system's design and the functionality necessary to deliver the value envisioned for the IT project has been provided. Quality means that the system delivered at the end of the project is fit for use and performs as defined by the user and documented by the project team.

An acceptable level of quality is achieved when a system's users put their hands on the keyboard and request a function or report and the system performs as anticipated and an appropriate output is provided. If users are able to fulfill their duties using the system in an intuitive, logical, and reasonably efficient manner, the project has been successful and a quality outcome has been achieved.

FIGURE 11.1 The Triple Constraint

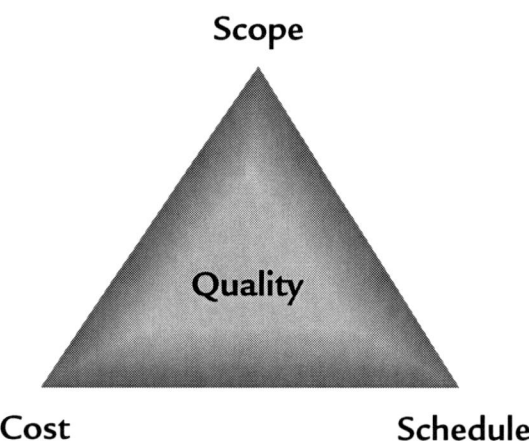

Poor quality can result in increased project costs through overt project failure and subsequent loss of investment, the cost of rework needed to correct deficiencies, job loss on the part of unsuccessful project teams, and opportunity loss when the sponsoring business is unable to capitalize on a business opportunity that the system would have supported.

Quality also is a measure of how well a project is carried out. Project quality refers to how well a project adheres to project management best practices. Those practices are identified in literature produced by organizations like the Project Management Institute, in its *Project Management Body of Knowledge* (4th edition). Project management best practices also can be gleaned from an organization's project management archives, where lessons learned are gathered from past projects and stored for future reference, as well as institutional guidelines and standards.

Q2 How do you monitor quality during an IT project?

Engineers define *quality* as meeting specifications; the product is designed and constructed as specified and is fit for use.

IT projects share many of the traits of traditional engineering projects. They use the same basic approach, from careful development of the product specifications to construction and finally testing of the end product to verify that it meets the customer's needs. Both IT and engineering projects rely on standards and guidelines to help with design and construction efforts, and both test products continuously throughout the project lifecycle.

When a software product is produced at the conclusion of a project and is found to meet specifications, including all appropriate guidelines and standards, that product is said to be of good quality.

Another way to look at project quality has less to do with product specifications and more to do with project management methodologies. The triple constraint suggests that a once a project's scope has been estimated and the work required to deliver that scope has been applied along a timeline, the resulting budget and schedule are inherently bound to the project's scope. If scope is changed, schedule and budget are impacted as well. If the schedule is curtailed, the ability of the project team to deliver the required scope is diminished.

With the complexities found in even the most simple of IT projects, few project sponsors would argue the notion that a quality project is one that provides the desired scope within the schedule and budget constraints defined for the project. Satisfying the triple constraint, then, defines a project management quality standard from the project sponsor's perspective.

A lack of quality can cost a project both time and money. Specific costs associated with this impact include:

- *The cost of rework*—The value of resources that must be acquired and consumed to redo work that should have been done correctly the first time.
- *The cost of project failure*—The need to write off the often-high cost of an IT project that failed to deliver its intended value to the organization.
- *Job loss*—The potential for members of a project team to lose their jobs because they have become associated with less-than-quality outcomes produced by their projects.
- *Opportunity loss*—The potential profit or other benefit that a company anticipated through delivery of a quality project, which must be written off because the project failed to provide its intended product.

Q3 What tools are used to manage quality for an IT project?

Quality is measured using metrics. Common metrics include measures of compliance with requirements, specifications, targets, standards, guidelines, and project objectives established for a project.

One measure of system quality can be related to the number of defects identified during testing. If standards, such as those imposed by law or organizational policy, apply to a project, another quality measure might address the degree of compliance with those standards. Metrics associated with project objectives measure the actual value provided by the project once it has been concluded, as compared with the value promised in project planning documentation.

Although quality can be measured manually, automated means are sometimes more efficient for capturing critical metrics. Lines of code generated for a project, for example, can be measured through automated tools that collect and catalog software development efforts carried out by the project team. System defect tracking and resolution rates are quality measures for which a host of automated tracking tools have been developed.

Whether tracked manually or with automated tools, quality measures should produce data that is easy to generate, read, and interpret. Figure 11.2 shows how defect tracking and resolution status is often reported for software development projects.

FIGURE 11.2 Sample Defect Tracking Log

Defect Tracking						
Rank (Open)	Finance	Accounts Receivable	Accounts Payable	Purchasing	General Ledger	Total
Severity 1	0	0	0	0	0	0
Severity 2	8	1	14	33	0	56
Severity 3	0	0	0	0	0	0
Severity 4	0	0	0	0	0	0
Severity 5	0	0	0	0	0	0
Total	8	1	14	33	0	56
Status						
Active	3	1	0	25	0	29
Resolved	5	0	8	8	0	21
Closed	0	0	6	0	0	6
Total	8	1	14	33	0	56

That same information can also be summarized graphically (Figure 11.3), an approach often preferred by senior management because of its ease of use.

FIGURE 11.3 Sample Graphic Display of Defect Tracking Progress

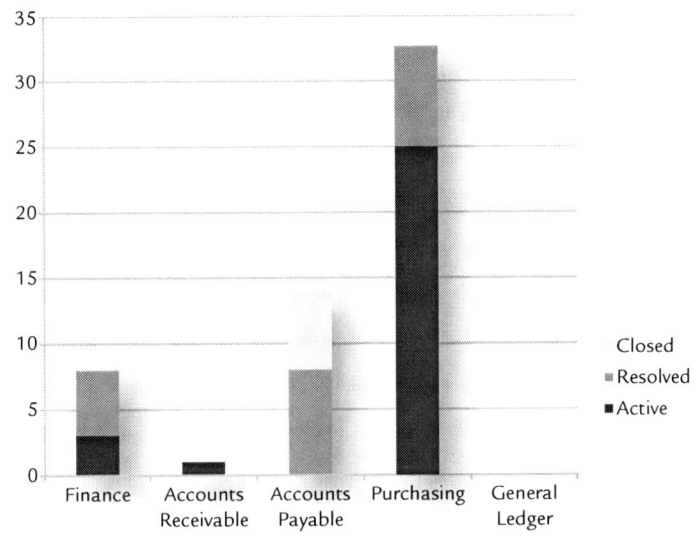

Q4 How do you assess the quality of software developed for an IT project?

It would be very challenging for a business-oriented project manager to check the quality of software developed by a project team. The project manager would lack the basic skills needed to make that sort of judgment. It would be nearly as difficult for a technically oriented project manager to complete the same task. The project manager of any reasonably complex project, whether a qualified technologist or a business professional, is usually too busy with day-to-day responsibilities to conduct any sort of detailed quality review of the software developed by a project team. A better approach would be to enlist a qualified technical resource to conduct a software code review.

The results of a code review can provide value to the team by identifying alternative strategies for software development and alternative methods for efficient data management. Code reviews can be conducted by other software developers at the unit level, or by the project's technical leader or system architect once the units of software have been integrated. The goal of a code review is to put another, objective set of eyes on the product to ensure it meets specifications and complies with the guidelines and standards set for the project.

Testing is another great determiner of software quality. Unit testing, the first level of this testing, provides a valuable tool for validating that the initial round of software development meets user specifications. Other forms of testing, including integration, system, performance, and user acceptance testing, also provide specific indicators of the quality of a project's deliverable software.

Q5 How do defects relate to an IT solution's quality?

A defect is some aspect of a product that does not meet specifications. Defects are normally uncovered during testing, but they might become apparent at any point in a project's development. Defects detract from the overall quality of the solution.

Software projects often generate a large numbers of defects during testing, and this results in many raised eyebrows from potential system users and project sponsors. These great numbers can often be attributed to the massive volume of code generated for the average software system as well as the complexity of the hardware that accompanies most technical solutions.

With millions of lines of software, it is virtually impossible to have everything line up perfectly the first time out. Defects should be expected. The number of defects identified for a project should not necessarily be interpreted as a measure of product quality. The fact that defects are uncovered and resolved before a new IT solution is implemented is an indicator of good project quality.

Q6 What is the best way to manage defects found during an IT project?

A key to IT project quality lies in how well the project team manages system defects during development and testing. Given the potentially large number of defects occurring on any IT project, the focus of the project team becomes how to best ensure those defects are appropriately managed. Defects that significantly impact project quality should be clearly identified and resolved. Other minor defects that might not affect system function or impact the business of the owning organization may be resolved as time and budget allow or perhaps not at all. If a defect does not impact the system's ability to support the business needs of the user, there might be no need to fix it and incur the cost of the rework.

The ability to prioritize defects is an important element of a project's defect management process. It enables project team members to rework system defects in order of importance, and it rationalizes a situation that can be perceived as overwhelming because of the sheer number of defects identified on some projects.

A defect prioritization schema should be well defined, understood by all members of the team, and validated by the project sponsor to ensure it aligns with that person's perception of the system's importance to the organization. One approach to categorizing defects by level of importance includes the following priorities:

- *Severity 1*—A system error that causes the system to crash and become nonfunctional. These defects must be addressed immediately.

- *Severity 2*—A system error that impacts a business process and for which no workaround exists. These defects must be corrected prior to acceptance of the system by the user.
- *Severity 3*—A system error that impacts a business process but for which a satisfactory workaround exists. These defects should be corrected prior to acceptance of the system by the user, but they may be deferred to a later phase of the project, if necessary.
- *Severity 4*—A system error that causes minor user inconvenience, which should be corrected but may be deferred.
- *Severity 5*—All other discrepancies. These defects may be deferred indefinitely.

Q7 Who defines quality for an IT project—the users or the technical team?

IT projects are undertaken to provide business value to the sponsoring organization. The individuals who are most knowledgeable of the business of the organization are best qualified to define what quality means for any IT product or solution.

Although the business owners are best positioned to determine what quality means for an IT project, it takes a team to deliver a quality IT solution. The project team's role on a project is to deliver the business value envisioned by the project sponsor. They bring their expertise to the project and work with the business analysts and users to design the business value envisioned by the project sponsor into the new solution.

The technical team plays an important role in achieving quality by ensuring that the technical requirements of the project are met. Those technical requirements might not appear obvious to the business side of the project team, but they are critical to the project's success. It would be poor quality, indeed, if a new solution was constructed and failed to meet user expectations because some technical aspect of the solution's design had gone unaddressed.

Q8 How do you convince a project sponsor to invest in quality when budgets are tight?

Quality costs money. If the approved scope is to be realized for an IT project, it will require an investment of time and capital. Unfortunately, there often is not enough money to go around and the quality of a project can be challenged.

The most direct way to secure a project sponsor's investment in a project's quality is to demonstrate the cost of not achieving quality. The potential costs of poor quality include:

- *Cost of rework*—Resources expended to fix avoidable defects and resolve other project-related problems.
- *Opportunity loss*—Costs associated with not seizing an opportunity to stimulate more revenue, reduce operational costs, or otherwise realize a potential benefit as a result of poor-quality project and product outcomes.
- *Project failure*—Costs associated with the failure of an IT project, which must be written off as a result of the project team's not delivering an acceptable technical solution and not meeting the organization's business needs.
- *Job loss*—More and more jobs are on the line because of project success or failure. Organizations cannot afford to invest in projects, or the people who run them, that cannot deliver successful project outcomes. Senior executives find themselves held increasingly accountable for project investments that do not meet an organization's expectations.

Chapter 12

HUMAN RESOURCE MANAGEMENT

All the great project management tools in the world will not deliver a successful IT project. It is people who complete the tasks that generate the deliverables that satisfy the user's needs.

Project teams consist of human resources who are assigned to the project by design, desire, and default. They come more or less skilled and carry all the enthusiasm, reservations, and baggage of any group of people stepping into a new position. The successful IT project manager appreciates this situation and plans for it. She relates to the need to align project team members with tasks best suited to their skills, and she understand that each project team member has unique needs that mean the difference between a highly successful project and one that does not satisfy its objectives.

Q1 How does human resource management relate to IT projects?

IT project human resource management deals with all things related to the people involved in an IT project.

People come in a multitude of varieties and forms. That very diversity can be both a benefit and a challenge for the IT project manager. Human resource management, as a discipline, enables project managers to assess and match human resources with the skill sets required to successfully deliver a project. It provides the tools needed to ensure the people on the project team have the capability and capacity to complete their assigned tasks in a manner that will enhance the opportunity for project success.

For human resource management to provide any value to a project, the project manager must first be in a position to identify the project's human resource requirements. The project's work plan, listing all the known project activities, must be in good enough shape to identify the type of work that will be carried out over the course of the project's schedule. From that list, the project manager can glean the skill sets necessary to complete the work as well as the potential number of team members required to get the work done in a reasonable period.

Once the skill sets have been identified, the project manager constructs a staffing management plan (Figure 12.1). This document identifies when each skill set is required over time and aligns those requirements with the available team member capabilities. The staff management plan enables the project manager to anticipate when specific project team members can be phased on or off the project. Software packages like Microsoft Project can provide excellent access to this information.

FIGURE 12.1 Sample Staffing Management Plan

Task #	Task	Start	Finish	Budget
	Host Committee Chair—Don Jones	April 20, 2009	June 30, 2011	2,940 hr.
1	Gather Lessons Learned from Sidney Convention	July 30, 2010	August 5, 2010	40 hr.
2	Build the Internal Roadshow	July 29, 2010	March 10, 2011	1,292 hr.
3	Establish a Command Post/Information Booth	June 24, 2011	June 30, 2011	40 hr.
4	Identify Your Message	May 15, 2009	January 1, 2010	1,328 hr.
5	Finance Committee Membership Identified	April 20, 2009	May 29, 2009	240 hr.

Good human resource management goes beyond identifying the resources and skill sets needed to complete a project. It digs deeper into the human element of the project and recognizes the need to build teams that function well together. It facilitates the development of project team members and subject matter experts so they can efficiently and effectively contribute to the project's success.

Seasoned IT project managers know that about 20 percent of all IT project time spent can be attributed to the technology used and developed for a project. The other 80 percent of project managers' time will be spent managing the dynamics of their human resources. Human resource management provides the tools necessary for the IT project manager to deal with those issues effectively.

Q2 Who provides the business and technical resources for an IT project?

Under ideal circumstances, it is the project manager and the project's technical lead who define the staffing needs for a project. Once they complete that task, they turn to the project sponsor to make the decision to commit and fund those resources for the project. From that perspective, the project sponsor is singularly responsible for securing the resources necessary to staff and complete an IT project.

Too often, project managers arrive on a job site to find that the project team members have already been assigned to the project. They find that the project sponsor, in his zeal for completing the project effectively, has assigned his best people to the team. Unfortunately, this is often done precipitously, without the benefit of a detailed skill set analysis. As a result, a gap might exist between the resources provided by the sponsor and the skill sets needed for the project. When this occurs, it is incumbent upon the project manager to build a clear case for filling the gap and deliver that message to the project sponsor. If the project manager lays out a sufficiently detailed case based on knowledge of the project, the project sponsor is likely to realize the mistake and fund the resources or training required to fill the gap.

Q3 What is a fat project team versus a lean project team?

Lean is a concept that stresses the need to realize maximum value and eliminate waste from any business process or project. A lean project team has on board at any time only those people who are integral to the work being completed by the project at that moment. All team members are productively engaged, with no one standing on the sidelines, killing time and wasting budget. Lean teams do not lack the full range of skill sets needed to complete the project's tasks, but they do not carry excess either.

Fat teams include team members who are not fully engaged at all times. Fat teams possess skill sets that might be considered overkill at any point in time on the project. Fat teams waste the project's budget by relying on overqualified resources and resources who are not fully engaged.

Consider a project team working on a custom software development project for a retail business. The project has completed project initiation and planning and is in the early stages of project execution. A software development vendor has been acquired and is working diligently without major complications. It will be another six months before testing can begin on the new software package.

The project team members listed in the first column of Figure 12.2 are assigned to the project fulltime. Considering the phase of the project and how things are going, an assessment of the project team might work out as shown in the other columns.

FIGURE 12.2 Sample Lean Team Analysis

Project Team Position	Necessary Resource?	Comment
Project manager	Yes	The project manager is the leader of the project's effort. A dedicated project manager is key to the success of a project of this type.

(continues)

(continued)

Project Team Position	Necessary Resource?	Comment
Technical architect	No	The technical architect is generally required early in the project and sporadically throughout the project. His work is completed when the architecture is defined. Full-time employment by the project is excessive.
Technical team leader	Yes	The technical team leader is the senior technical resource for the project. Her presence is required to ensure the vendor's deliverables meet project specifications and best practice standards.
Software developers	No	The vendor is providing the major software development effort. Internal resources assigned to the project team on a full-time basis would be redundant.
Business team leader	Yes	The business team leader is the senior business resource for the project. His presence is required to ensure the vendor's deliverables meet the business requirements specifications for the project.
Business analysts	No	Once the vendor contract has been awarded, most of the requirements definition has been completed for the project. The business analysts who did that work in the beginning might be needed occasionally to interpret their work for the vendor, but they are not required fulltime.
Database modeler	No	Database modeling, like business analysis, is done at the conceptual and logical level early in the project. This person might be required to interpret her early work for the vendor and project team, but she would not be required on a full-time basis during project execution.
Communications manager	Maybe	Depending on the sensitivity of the project, a communications manager might or might not be required fulltime. Good communications with stakeholders sink or support projects, so it is always good to err on the side of strong communications capabilities.
Contract manager	No	The contract manager is a key resource when a request for proposal is in development and during the vendor selection and contracting processes. Beyond that point, contracts personnel are on-call resources who should be available for consultation. Their presence is not usually required on a full-time basis.

The goal of any IT project manager should be to consume the minimum resources necessary to deliver the maximum possible value to the sponsoring organization. Fat teams should not be tolerated. People who are not engaged fully but take up space in a project office drag down the morale of those wrestling with the many intense and challenging issues that confront IT projects.

The project management lean rule of thumb: Never tolerate a fat team. Lean teams are agile and efficient, and they deliver successful projects.

Q4 How do you gain the support of nontechnical SMEs working on technical projects?

Successful IT projects require a blend of technical and nontechnical resources. Nontechnical subject matter experts (SMEs) provide critical information to the team about the business functions that are to be modeled or supported by the project's technical solution. Getting the technical side of the project to interact and talk effectively with SMEs, and vice versa, can sometimes be a chore.

The good news is that the days of IT-centric projects have pretty much faded into the past. Few organizations beyond those engaged purely in IT research and development, where the goal is to develop new technology for its own sake, carry out projects that can be classified as uniquely and solely IT in nature. Seasoned technical resources associated with successful IT projects understand this and appreciate the need to communicate with nontechnical SMEs at the business level.

By assigning experienced technical resources who appreciate this point of a project, and who possess good communication skills, most communications issues between technical teams and nontechnical SMEs can be resolved. Those resources bridge the divide between tech-speak and the nontechnical lay point of view so that the business experts can have their say and the technical team can collect and utilize the business experts' knowledge for the benefit of the project.

Q5 How do you hold team members accountable when you don't share the same skill sets?

Some people in the IT project management field feel that the best project managers are those with an in-depth business background, who can bring their understanding of the business's needs to the project. Others feel that for highly technical projects, it is the technical expertise that matters most, and effective project managers are those who have a deep technical background. It is doubtful that this question will be resolved anytime soon. Regardless of the answer, however, there is no easy way to hold project team members accountable for their work when the project manager is not intimate with each specific team member's skill set.

In the first case, the business-oriented project manager might lack sufficient technical background to evaluate technical effort and deliverables with any degree of confidence. Even if he takes courses in software development, database modeling, network design, and so on to increase his understanding, the chances of his staying current in any of those fields while working as a project manager are slim. Technology moves ahead too fast, and the demands of IT project management are often too great for that to be ensured with any certainty.

Similarly, the technically-oriented IT project manager effectively leaves the technical disciplines behind when called upon to manage an IT project of any size. As a result, her specific technology background quickly becomes dated, and she finds herself in a position similar to that of the business-oriented project manager.

The only viable solution for this situation is for IT project managers of all kinds to partner up with senior project team members who have the necessary expertise to augment the project managers' capabilities. The project managers can then delegate responsibility for team member evaluations to those persons.

If a project manager is unable to acquire the skill sets needed to fill his need for team oversight, another approach that can be used is independent validation and verification, or IV&V. IV&V teams are hired for brief periods to assess technical progress and completeness for IT projects. The teams can be configured with the necessary technical expertise to provide a thorough and objective assessment of technical team deliverables. Although this approach can be expensive, for highly complex projects where a good deal of money is on the line, the dispassionate perspective and potentially extensive repertoire of expertise of IV&V teams can provide a major benefit to the project manager and the project.

RISK MANAGEMENT

Chapter 13

An IT project, by its very nature, produces an automated system, infrastructure, tool, or other result that either did not exist before the project or was modified substantially as a result of the project. Something new is generated. The project teams and stakeholders enter into the project with an idea of what the end result will look like, but without the benefit of absolute knowledge.

On a good day, a project team can expect to fully grasp 85 to 90 percent of the requirements that must be met for a technology project. The balance remains unknown for the process of progressive elaboration and discovery. That remainder, that unknown, is referred to as risk. The smart project manager and team wrestle with that risk in a process known as risk management. The outcome of the process is a best attempt at understanding what the project's future might bring, both good and not-so-good.

Q1 What is risk management and how does it relate to IT project management?

Risk management includes the planning and implementation of processes for identifying, assessing, and managing risks that might impact an IT project. Risk management allows project teams to anticipate what might go wrong with a project and, occasionally, how a positive benefit might be realized if uncertain events come to pass. It is an organized approach for glancing into the future, dipping the project's toe into water that is otherwise unknown, and preparing for eventualities associated with that experience.

A risk is any potential event that could impact a project on a quantitative or qualitative basis. Risks are identified in terms of the nature and focus of the event (loss of key human resources, catastrophic system failure, etc.), the probability of its occurrence (identified quantitatively as a degree of probability or percentage), and the potential impact on the project.

The impact of a risk can be positive (beneficial) or negative (bad), and it can be qualitative or quantifiable. A positive impact might suggest that if something happens, the project might save budget or schedule. A negative impact could be the reverse and cost the project additional time or money.

Qualitative impacts on projects include such things as loss of team morale or negative implications for the organization's reputation. Qualitative impacts are difficult to measure but are important because they can stimulate other, more quantitative, non–project-related impacts on the organization carrying out the project.

A risk's quantitative impact can be measured. Most typical quantitative impacts are expressed as impact on budget or schedule. For example, project cost overruns (measured in dollars) and schedule delays (measured in units of time) are often realized from risks that thus are considered quantitative in nature.

The goal of risk management is to identify risks early in a project's life cycle, assess their potential impacts, and develop management strategies for the risks of greatest importance to the project.

Q2 What is included in a risk management plan for an IT project?

The table of contents for an IT project's risk management plan commonly includes the following elements:

- *Risk Management Goals and Objectives*—A statement of the goals and objectives of the risk management program for the project
- *Roles and Responsibilities*—An itemization of the members of the project management team who are responsible for managing risk on the project
- *Risk Management Approach*, including:
  - Risk management strategies
  - Risk management processes, including:
    - Risk identification
    - Qualitative and quantitative risk analysis
    - Risk response planning
    - Risk monitoring
    - Risk control
- *Risk Management Tools*—A list of tracking tools and techniques that will be used to collect and track project risks
- *Contingency Calculation*—Processes for calculating cost and schedule contingency requirements
- Other comments provided by the project manager.

Q3 What risks are commonly faced by IT projects?

Some of the more common risks and risk management strategies associated with IT projects are described in Figure 13.1.

FIGURE 13.1 Common IT Project Risks

Potential Risk
Senior Management Involvement
Inadequate top management, sponsorship, and support results in decision-making that is not timely, which has a high probability of negatively impacting project schedule.
Stakeholder Commitment
Lack of internal and external stakeholder commitment results in the omission of key requirements during the project planning phase, which will require eventual rework, negatively impacting both schedule and cost.
Expectations Management
Constituent and stakeholder expectations do not match the project vision, goals, and objectives. The resulting conflict detracts from project progress, potentially impacting project schedule and cost.
Project Team Experience
Limited large-scale project experience within the project team results in project delays as team members are trained and additional resources are brought onto the team to augment the experience deficit. This potentially impacts project cost and schedule.
Change Management
Inadequate change management processes needed to prepare the organization(s) to implement the new program delay implementation of the technical solution, resulting in schedule delays.
Test Management
Inadequate testing process for automated systems results in unidentified and unresolved system defects. This will stimulate rework and negatively impact project schedule and cost.
Organizational Commitment
Internal or external priorities within the sponsoring organization compete with the project for key business and technical resources. This risk might negatively impact project schedule and, if external resources must be hired to augment the project team, project cost.

(continues)

(continued)

Potential Risk
Scope Management
Lack of adequate scope management processes allows undocumented changes to the project's original vision and objectives. Scope creep is encountered, potentially impacting project scope, schedule, and cost.
Resource Availability
Lack of qualified project resources results in project tasks being completed late and stimulates the need to acquire external project resources. This could negatively impact project schedule and cost.
Schedule Constraints
Constrained project delivery timelines impose unrealistic timeframes on project team performance. This might negatively impact the project team's ability to deliver the full project scope.
Resource Stability
The departure of key resources during the project results in a lack of expertise late in the project's life cycle. This might stimulate the need to acquire additional resources, orient them to the project's requirements, and ramp up their work effort to match team needs. This will potentially impact both project schedule and cost.

Q4 Who is the best person to manage risks for an IT project?

The project manager carries the burden and responsibility for managing project risks. It is the project manager who sets the tone for all project team activities, and risk management sits atop that list in terms of importance and potential benefit to the project.

Every member of the project team shares responsibility for risk management. The project manager may assign a risk to any member of the project team for monitoring and management, but all team members should be familiar with risk management and be on the watch for risks that might impact the project's opportunity for success.

Q5 What tools are used to track and manage IT project risks?

The two dominant and most effective tools used to manage risks on an IT project are the risk management plan and the risk tracking log. A risk tracking log (Figure 13.2)

FIGURE 13.2 Sample Risk Tracking Log

Risk #	Description	Qualitative or Quantitative Risk	Priority 1–5	Likeli-hood %	Potential Impact	Risk Management Strategy	Risk Response Plan	Assigned To	Status
1	Key staff will be lost from the project and must be replaced. If this risk occurs, there will be an impact on the schedule when a replacement is trained and brought up to speed.	Quantitative	1	90%	4 weeks and $20,000	Mitigate	Identify potential candidates for replacing the key staff member in advance.	Human resource manager	Open
2	The technology vendor might go out of business due to the poor economy. Locating a backup vendor and placing orders will delay the schedule by 9 weeks and cost an additional $50,000 due to increased costs.	Quantitative	2	40%	8 weeks and $50,000	Mitigate	Identify backup vendor and preposition purchase requests in the event the primary vendor's business fails.	Purchasing lead	Open
3	Delays in delivery of the technical solution will result in loss of reputation for the organization and potential ill will with the organization's customers.	Qualitative	3	25%	Loss of goodwill with customers	Avoid	Implement a good communications plan to set appropriate expectations with customers and ensure they are kept abreast of all issues associated with the customer; demonstrate goodwill and full transparency.	Project manager	Open

captures the following information pertaining to project risks, which the project team can use to anticipate challenges the project might face in the future:

- *Risk number*—Sequentially number the risks as they are entered into the log, for ease of reference.
- *Description*—Very briefly identify the risk in terms of the risk's area of focus and its potential impact on the project.
- *Qualitative or quantitative risk*—Indicate whether the risk is one where the impact can be measured objectively or whether it has a potential qualitative impact. A qualitative impact might be something such as the organization's goodwill being damaged by the project or the morale of the project team being diminished. A quantitative impact would include specific delays to the schedule or impact on the budget.
- *Priority*—Assess the risk's importance to the project. This is a judgment call on the part of the project team, factoring in the probability of occurrence and impact, stated in quantitative or qualitative terms. A risk with a very high probability of occurrence and significant potential impact on the project's scope, schedule, and cost would be rated as a high priority.
- *Likelihood of occurrence*—State in terms of the probability of the risk's manifesting at some point in the future. Often, organizations rate this as a high, medium, or low likelihood of occurrence. However, those terms are difficult to define and might mean different things to different people.
- *Potential impact*—For quantifiable risks, identify the impact on the schedule in units of time (hours, days, weeks, etc.). Identify impact on the budget as a discrete dollar value. Often, organizations rate this as a high, medium, or low impact on the project. As with assessing likelihood of occurrence, the terms are difficult to define and might mean different things to different people. For qualitative impacts, specify the nature of the impact in appropriate, subjective terms.
- *Risk management strategy*—Specify the strategy for managing risk. Commonly used strategies are avoidance, mitigation, acceptance, and transfer of the risk.
- *Risk response plan*—Elaborate on the risk management strategy, spelling out the specific steps that should be taken by the project team should the risk manifest.
- *Responsibility*—Specify the person on the project team assigned to track the risk. This should be the person most closely associated with the element of the project that would be impacted by the risk.
- *Status of the risk*—State as either open or retired. Risks remain open for as long as they are active. Once the potential for the risk has passed, it can be retired and removed from the risk management log.
- *Last update*—Enter the date the risk was last reviewed by the project team. Use this field to ensure risks are kept current through the life of the project.

Q6 How is risk management used to calculate contingency requirements for an IT project?

Risk-based contingency analysis (RBCA) provides an objective approach to calculating budget and schedule contingency requirements for IT projects. If a risk management log has been maintained as described in the previous chapter, the quantifiable risks provide the information needed to identify contingency needs for a project.

To complete an RBCA, the project manager extracts the information needed for the analysis from the project's risk management log. From that log, the project manager captures the risk identification number, probability of occurrence, and impact for each quantifiable risk and then inserts it into a spreadsheet configured as depicted in Figure 13.3.

FIGURE 13.3 Sample Risk-Based Contingency Analysis

Risk Number	Likelihood %	Potential Impact	Weighted Value
1	90%	4 weeks and $20,000	18 days and $18,000
2	40%	8 weeks and $50,000	16 days and $20,000
3	25%	Loss of goodwill with customers	Not applicable
4	40%	4 weeks and $10,000	8 days and $4,000
5	35%	8 weeks and $10,000	14 days and $3,500
6	60%	2 weeks	6 days
7	50%	$60,000	$30,000
8	25%	5 weeks and $20,000	6 days and $5,000
9	30%	2 weeks and $5,000	3 days and $1,500
10	45%	2 weeks and $10,000	5 days and $4,500
11	50%	3 weeks and $50,000	8 days and $25,000
12	75%	2 weeks and $20,000	8 days and $15,000
Contingency requirement			92 days and $126,500

The analysis is completed by multiplying the probability of the risk's occurring with the potential schedule and cost impact for each quantifiable risk. The result is a set of weighted values that can be totaled to determine the total schedule and budget contingency requirements for the project.

It is important to know that this method of computing contingency requirements for an IT project assumes that the chance of any risk's occurring and the estimated impact of that risk's being felt, in total or in part, is a probability and not a certainty. Based on that assumption, each risk and its associated impacts represent some fraction of the potential total impact that might be realized by the project. Assigning weighted values to each risk allows the project manager to factor that level of uncertainty into the calculation without assigning an inappropriately high or low level of significance to any single risk identified in the log.

RBCA has several major advantages for IT project managers and their teams. The first benefit is that the math is relatively easy to do. The second is that RBCA is based on math that can be explained and supported by the project team's thorough risk analysis.

In some cases, IT project teams determine contingency based on their best feel for the situation, a subjective estimate based on prior experience. In other cases, analogous projects are identified and the contingency needs identified for those projects are used as a starting point for estimating contingency needs for the current project. Neither approach is bad in and of itself. When money gets tight, however, business managers and executives often feel the need for something more substantive that goes beyond a best guess or subjective assessment before they are willing to set aside thousands of dollars and months of staff time as contingency. RBCA meets that need and provides an approach that can be supported in terms that business executives can understand and appreciate.

Chapter 14

PROCUREMENT MANAGEMENT

More IT projects are contracted out today than ever before. Business and agency staffs have become more lean than in years past as those entities have wrestled with uncertain markets and tax bases. Agencies and businesses no longer have the technical and support staff to spare for large project teams, and they cannot afford to train and maintain staffs of qualified IT project managers. As a result, they contract out IT projects in total or in part. It is an act of convenience that makes good business sense but also carries a certain degree of risk.

Q1 What is procurement management planning and why is it so important for IT projects?

Procurement management planning addresses the acquisition of services and things needed to complete an IT project. It may include the purchase of hardware, software, consultant services, project management, and personal services of all types. The discipline of procurement management planning includes all the processes needed to plan and execute procurement transactions for an IT project.

The procurement management process includes developing and executing a plan that addresses the following topics:

- Identifying which project needs can best be met by purchasing or acquiring products, services, or results outside the project organization
- Developing plans for defining procurement requirements
- Identifying potential sources for the required goods or services
- Publishing requests for proposal or quote to initiate the procurement process
- Identifying and selecting the best value offered by responding vendors
- Awarding a contract for the purchase
- Monitoring and controlling procurement activity from planning to delivery of the product or completion of the services
- Closing out the procurement activity.

Q2 Which comes first—the request for proposal or the procurement management plan?

Requests for proposal (RFP) and requests for quote (RFQ) are tools developed to execute an IT project's procurement strategy. From that standpoint, it is essential that the plan precede the RFP or RFQ. Doing so ensures that those documents benefit from the project team's deliberate consideration of the project's full range of procurement needs and how best to go about meeting those needs. Without engaging the procurement planning process, opportunities might be overlooked to bundle procurements, achieve economies of scale, or manage highly risky procurements with the detail necessary to ensure success.

Q3 Why do IT projects have so many contractors, who come and go, on the project team?

IT project resources can be costly commodities. Many organizations deliberately bring them on to support a project and cut them loose when the need has passed to avoid the cost of maintaining those resources on staff when they are not otherwise needed. It is good economics in an industry notorious for its high human resource costs.

Planning the acquisition and release of contract resources for an IT project is similar to planning the assignment and release of project resources acquired from within the organization. Project tasks are identified and scheduled; resources are assigned; and, in the case where resources are not available from within for any reason, those needs are contracted from outside the organization.

It is important to remember that contractors are people who have needs and complexities similar to those of the resources assigned to a project team from within the organization. When they come onto a project, contractors need time to ramp up their knowledge and understand the project's vision, objectives, and team culture. As they prepare to depart, they need to pass on their knowledge to those who will remain behind. Time should be programmed for contractors to accomplish these tasks, just as it is for internally acquired project resources.

Q4 Is it okay for an outside contractor to manage an IT project for an organization?

Organizations commonly contract for the services of IT project managers. Those agencies and firms might do IT projects on a relatively infrequent basis. In such circumstances, it makes sense to bring on transient resources to fill the skill set void when an IT project is being considered. Retaining qualified IT project managers on staff during the long periods between IT projects would be costly and make little sense.

When a contract project manager is assigned to manage an IT project for an organization, it is critical that the person work directly for the business manager or executive for whom the system will be implemented. That reporting relationship ensures that the organization's goals and objectives are appropriately considered by the project manager and enforced by someone organic to the organization. It also provides an opportunity for timely decision-making when matters of organizational policy that are beyond the purview of the contract project manager must be addressed.

Q5 How do you verify that your contractors have the skills they say they have?

Anyone can craft a resume or business brief that looks good, but it is not until the task is at hand that we often fully understand a resource's true abilities. Four major approaches can help ensure a contract resource has the skills needed for a project:

- *Reference checks*—Require that a candidate provide contact information for people for whom he has worked and used the skills needed for the project. Call those references and get their opinion of how well the resource performed on their project. Beware of contacts who refuse to provide a reference; this is tantamount to saying that the resource performed poorly in the past.

- *Certifications*—Numerous types of technical and nontechnical certifications are available for potential project resources, including those offered by Microsoft, the Software Engineering Institute, the Project Management Institute, and others. Requiring proof of certification is a good way to determine whether a candidate has at least enough education and experience to pass a certification exam. Note that certification is not the final determinant for whether a person is qualified for a job. It does indicate that the candidate has gone to the trouble of studying a specific aspect of software design, development, or project management to the extent that she can pass a comprehensive examination.

- *Technical skill tests*—Many organizations are resorting to hands-on testing of resource skill sets. It is common for a person applying for an administrative assistant position to be tested for his ability to use common office software to prepare correspondence, complete email, and set up a simple spreadsheet. Why not ask a software developer to construct an object, analyze a database model, or troubleshoot a small system? If the test is set up by a knowledgeable professional, it can provide excellent insight regarding the candidate's potential as a skilled project team member.

- *Communication skills tests*—Many people say they can write, run a meeting, or relate to others in a group setting. Unfortunately, those are often the most challenging skills to find in potential IT project team members. Education standards around the world vary greatly, and the diversity of our culture, while offering a great opportunity to provide multiple perspectives for any problem, can create language barriers. It is essential that any potential member of a project team, and in particular those who will lead the project or a portion of the team, have good communication skills.

Be sure to test communication skills before hiring or contracting for a resource by asking candidates to compose a short letter on a laptop computer or provide copies of written deliverables for the selection board to review. Engage the candidate in an impromptu discussion and assess her ability to speak thoughtfully and clearly on a variety of topics. Rate the candidate's performance in these areas, and develop a record of the candidates with communication skills that will benefit the project.

When considering contract resources for an IT project, look to each of the approaches described above to weed out the qualified candidates from those who might not have what it takes to help the team to be successful.

Q6 What performance standards should be defined as part of a contract for IT services?

Performance standards come in many sizes and shapes, and all should be considered for use in contract documents for products and personal services. Some of the performance standards commonly included in contracts established for IT projects include:

- *Project performance standards*—The intended adherence to project management best practices. This standard should reference the specific source of those best practices as well as any tolerance for variance in a project's cost and schedule constraints as defined by the sponsoring organization.
- *Software performance standards*—The software's desired performance attributes and functionality.
- *Hardware performance standards*—Characteristics and performance attributes of the hardware required or available to support a system, network, or infrastructure.

Without performance standards in place in a contract, potential vendors have no benchmark against which their performance can be compared to determine whether they were successful. Project teams would have no standard against which to measure a vendor's project deliverables to determine their acceptability.

Sources for performance standards include organization policies and guidelines, expert judgment, engineering standards, existing systems, and user experience.

BIBLIOGRAPHY

The following books are excellent sources of information for IT project management information. Much of the information provided in this book is elaborated in the references provided below.

Budd, Charles, and Charlene Budd. 2010. *A Practical Guide to Earned Value Project Management*. Vienna, VA: Management Concepts.

Fleming, Quentin. 2003. *Project Procurement Management: Contracting, Subcontracting, Teaming*. Tustin, CA: FMC Press.

Furman, Jeff. 2011. *The Project Management Answer Book*. Vienna, VA: Management Concepts.

Hillson, David, and Peter Simon. 2007. *Practical Risk Management, the ATOM Methodology*. Vienna, VA: Management Concepts.

Johnson, Jim. 2006. *My Life is Failure: 100 Things You Should Know to Be a Successful Project Leader*. West Yarmouth, MA: The Standish Group International.

Kaydos, Will. 1998. *Operational Performance Measurement: Increasing Total Productivity*. New York: T. Lucie Press.

Kliem, Ralph. 2008. *Effective Communications for Project Management*. New York: Auerbach Publications.

Kotter, John. 1996. *Leading Change*. Boston: Harvard Business School Press.

Mulcahy, Rita. 2009. *PM Crash Course for IT Professionals: Real-World Project Management Tools and Techniques for IT Initiatives*. Minnetonka, MN: RMC Publications, Inc.

Phillips, Dwayne. 1998. *The Software Project Manager's Handbook: Principles that Work at Work*. Piscataway, NJ: IEEE Computer Society Press.

Pratt, David. 2010. *Pragmatic Project Management: Five Scalable Steps to Success*. Vienna, VA: Management Concepts.

Rose, Kenneth. 2005. *Project Quality Management: Why, What and How*. Boca Raton, FL: J. Ross Publishing.

Schiesser, Rich. 2002. *IT Systems Management: Designing, Implementing, and Managing World Class Infrastructures*. Upper Saddle River, NJ: Prentice Hall.

Stratton, Ray. 2006. *The Earned Value Management Maturity Model*. Vienna, VA: Management Concepts.

Wong, Zachary. 2007. *Human Factors in Project Management: Concepts, Tools, and Techniques for Inspiring Teamwork and Motivation*. San Francisco: Josey-Bass.

Young, Ralph. 2006. *Project Requirements: A Guide to Best Practices*. Vienna, VA: Management Concepts.

INDEX

A
abbreviated testing, 108
actual cost (AC), 128
Agile project delivery, 58–62
architectural tests, 124

B
budget information, 156–157
business analysis, 69–70
business analysts, 27
business architecture, 62–64
business case, 48–50
business team leader, 28
business team members, 29–30

C
change management, 98–99
closeout
   activities, 110–113
   beginning, 109–110
   documenting, 114
   leading, 113
   project archive, 113–114
   report, 114–117
CM. *See* configuration management
code reviews, 123
commercial off-the-shelf (COTS), 13
communications management, 38
communications manager role, 39
conceptual data model, 84

configuration management (CM), 71, 98
configuration manager, 39
contract resources, 158
contractor skills, 182–184
cost management
   budget information, 156–157
   Budget Planning Checklist, 156–157
   communications, 154
   contract resources, 158
   employee benefits, 154
   hardware maintenance, 155
   hardware rent/lease, 155
   other costs, 155
   overhead, 155
   personal service contracts, 154
   problems, 153–154
   risks, 157–158
   salaries and wages, 154
   software maintenance and upgrade, 155
   software rent/lease, 155
   tracking costs, 155–156
   travel, 155
costs, tracking, 155–156
COTS. *See* commercial off-the-shelf
COTS implementation, 30, 32
COTS integration, 30, 32
COTS package implementation project, 33
custom software development, 12, 30, 32

D

data migration, 65–66
database design
   conceptual data model, 84
   logical data model, 85
   modeling, 83–84
   physical database, 85
   planning phase, 82–83
defect log, 105–108
defect management, 104–105, 162
defects, 164–165
deliverables
   definition, 48
   new system requirements, 75–77
   project management plan, 77–79
   project planning process, 74–75
   Sample Detailed Requirements in Conceptual View, 77

E

earned value (EV), 128
earned value analysis (EVA), 120, 127–128
employee benefits, 154

F

fat project teams, 169–171
feasibility study, 50–51
functional design development, 57

H

hardware maintenance, 155
hardware rent/lease, 155
human resource (HR), 47
human resource management
   accountability, 171–172
   business and technical resources, 168–169
   importance of, 167–168
   nontechnical subject matter experts, 171
   Simple Staffing Plan, 168

I

implementation team leader, 29

independent verification and validation (IV&V), 22, 92
infrastructure project, 13
infrastructure upgrade, 30, 34, 36
IT project manager role, 37
IT project status report, 121
IV&V. *See* independent verification and validation

L

leaders, 28
leadership teams, 15–16
lean project teams, 169–171
logical data model, 85

M

manuals, 104
meetings, types of, 96–97
modeling, database design, 83–84
monitoring and control
   architectural tests, 124
   code reviews, 123
   earned value analysis, 127–128
   IT project status report, 121
   levels of control, 125–127
   project managers lacking technical skills, 121–123
   Project Status Report Template, 122
   stakeholder expectations, 124–125
   tools, 119–120

N

network architecture, 65
new system requirements, 75–77

O

organization
   leadership team, 15–16
   Project Advisory Group, 16
   project manager reporting, 16–18
   Project Sponsor/Project Manager Relationship, 16
   Project Steering Committee, 16
overhead, 155

P

performance standards, 184
personal service contracts, 154
physical database, 85
planned value (PV), 128
procurement management
    contractor skills, 182–184
    performance standards, 184
    planning, 181
    requests for proposal, 182
    requests for quote, 182
project archive, 113–114
project charter
    content, 52–53
    definition, 51–52
    deliverables, 53
    requirements, 54
project control, 94–95
project execution
    abbreviated testing, 108
    beginning, 87–88
    change management, 98–99
    configuration management, 98
    defect log, 105–108
    defect management, 104–105
    deliverables, 102–103
    independent verification and
        validation, 92
    leading, 88
    manuals, 104
    meetings, types of, 96–97
    project control, 94–95
    Project Execution Checklist, 89–91
    project team meetings, 95–96
    system readiness assessment, 99–101
    technical design documents, 93
    testing, 104
    training, 104
    user involvement, 92
project initiation process
    project objectives, 46–47
    skill sets, 44–45
    tasks, 43–44
    vision statement, 45–46

project management
    communications management, 38
    communications manager role, 39
    configuration manager, 39
    experience, importance of, 8–9
    filling project manager void, 8
    IT project manager role, 37
    Project Scaling Guide, 11
    project size, 11–12
    Simple n-Tier Architecture Diagram, 40
    skills, 9–11
    subject matter experts, 41
    technical architect, 39–41
    technical resources as managers, 7–8
    technologists *versus* business people, 37
    test management, 38
    test manager role, 38
project management plan, 77–79
project planning
    Agile IT Project Work Plan, 63
    Agile Process Capability Map, 60
    Agile Process Summary, 61
    Agile project delivery, 58–60
    business analysis, 69–70
    business architecture, 62–64
    Business Architecture Trace to System
        Requirements, 64
    Common IT Project Risks, 70–74
    data migration, 65–66
    Data Migration Plan Checklist, 66
    functional design development, 57
    High-Level Business Architecture, 64
    IT Waterfall Approach, 59
    Linear Project Management Life
        Cycle, 55
    network architecture, 65
    overview, 55–57
    project status reports, 66–67
    Realistic Project Management Life Cycle,
        56
    requirements traceability, 67–69
    Requirements Traceability
        Template, 69
    risk, 70–74

Simple Project Status Report
  Template, 68
 types, 57–58
 users, including, 62
project planning process, 74–75
project size, 11–12
project status reports, 66–67
project team meetings, 95–96
project teams
 business analysts, 27
 business team leader, 28
 business team members, 29–30
 Common Role by Position, 20
 COTS implementation, 30, 32
 COTS integration, 30, 32
 COTS Project Team Organization, 33
 customer software development, 30, 32
 implementation team leader, 29
 infrastructure upgrade, 30, 34, 36
 Infrastructure Upgrade Project
  Organization, 36
 IT Project Team Roles and
  Responsibilities, 21–25
 Large IT Project Organization, 31
 leaders, 28
 quality assurance analysts, 36–37
 resources, 18
 roles and responsibilities, 18
 skill sets, 18
 software developers, 27
 system modernization, 30, 32, 34
 System Modernization Project
  Organization, 34
 technical team, 27
 technical team leader, 29
 transfer system, 30, 32
 Typical IT Project Team Organization, 19
 vendor roles and responsibilities, 25–26
project types
 COTS package implementation project, 13
 custom software development project, 12
 infrastructure project, 13
 IT *versus* business-oriented, 12
 software package integration project, 13

 transfer system project, 13–14
PV. *See* planned value

Q
quality assurance (QA), 36
quality assurance analysts, 36–37
quality management
 assessing software quality, 163
 Defect Tracking Log, 162
 defects, 164–165
 defining quality, 165
 investing in quality, 165–166
 monitoring, 160–161
 planning for, 159–160
 tools, 161–163
 Triple Constraint, 159

R
RBCA. *See* risk-based contingency analysis
reporting, project manager, 16–18
requests for proposal (RFP), 182
requests for quote (RFQ), 182
requirements, 54
requirements traceability, 67–69
resources, 18
return on investment (ROI), 155
RFP. *See* requests for proposal
RFQ. *See* requests for quote
risk management
 Common IT Project Risks, 175–176
 contingency requirements, 179–180
 cost management, 157–158
 definition, 173–174
 plan, 174
 project manager responsibilities, 176
 project planning, 70–74
 tools, 176–178
risk-based contingency analysis (RBCA),
  179
ROI. *See* return on investment
roles and responsibilities, project teams, 18

S
salaries and wages, 154

scope management
- change approval authority, 137
- Change Control Form Template, 132
- defining scope, 129–130
- deliverables, 134
- encouraging initiative, 130–131
- late-stage change requests, 136
- optimization, 131–133
- scope creep, 134–136
- use cases, 134–135

skills
- contractor, 182–184
- project initiation, 44–45
- project management, 9–11
- project teams, 18

SME. *See* subject matter expert
software developers, 27
software maintenance and upgrade, 155
software package integration project, 13
software rent/lease, 155
stakeholder expectations, 124–125
subject matter expert (SME), 24, 29, 41, 171

success factors
- business value, 5–6
- key indicators, 2–5
- Project Scaling Model, 6–7
- Project Success Assessment Matrix, 3–4
- risk, 1–2

system modernization, 30, 32, 34
system readiness assessment, 99–101

T

technical architect, 39–41
technical design documents, 93
technical resources as managers, 7–8
technical team, 27
technical team leader, 29
test management, 38
test manager role, 38

test planning
- documentation, 82
- integration testing, 80
- performance testing, 81
- regression testing, 81–82
- system testing, 80
- unit testing, 80
- user acceptance testing, 81

testing, 80–82, 104

time management
- activities, comparing by project type, 144–148
- developing schedules, 139–144
- requirements traceability, 148
- risks, 149–152
- schedule management, 159

tools, monitoring and control, 119–120
training, 104
transfer system project, 13–14, 30, 32
travel, 155
triple constraint, 159

U

user acceptance testing (UAT), 81
user involvement, project execution, 92

V

vendor roles and responsibilities, 25–26

Complement Your Project Management Library with These Additional Resources from
MANAGEMENTCONCEPTPRESS

The Complete Project Manager: Integrating People, Organizational, and Technical Skills
Randall Englund and Alfonso Bucero

This book integrates theory and application, humor and passion, and concepts and examples drawn from the authors' experiences as well as from contributors who share their stories. The concepts are easy to understand, universal, powerful, and readily applicable. There is no complicated model to understand before practicing what you learn…or wish you had learned when starting your career.

ISBN 978-1-56726-359-6 ■ Product Code B596 ■ 286 pages

The Project Management Coaching Workbook: Six Steps to Unleashing Your Potential
Susanne Madsen

Starting with an insightful self-assessment, this book offers tools, questions, reviews, guiding practices, and exercises that will help you build your roadmap to project management and leadership success. Based on her experience as a coach and mentor, Susanne Madsen offers a proven six-step method designed to help you understand and articulate what you want to achieve—and then assist you in achieving those goals.

ISBN 978-1-56726-357-2 ■ Product Code B572 ■ 236 pages

Interpersonal Skills for Portfolio, Program, and Project Managers
Ginger Levin, DPA, PMP, PgMP

Any formula for management success must include a high level of interpersonal skills. The growing complexity of organizational portfolios, programs, and projects, as well as the increasing number and geographic dispersion of stakeholders and employees, makes a manager's interpersonal skills critical. The frequency and variety of interpersonal interactions and the pressure to perform multiple leadership roles successfully while ensuring customer satisfaction have never been greater. This book offers practical and proven tools and methods you can use to develop your interpersonal skills and meet the challenges of today's competitive professional environment.

ISBN 978-1-56726-288-9 ■ Product Code B889 ■ 286 pages

The Project Management Answer Book
Jeff Furman, PMP

This easy-to-use Q&A reference covers all aspects of project management and includes practical tips on obtaining the PMP and related certifications. This book provides you with the tools you need to improve project performance and achieve high-quality, low-risk results immediately.

ISBN 978-1-56726-297-1 ■ Product Code B971 ■ 416 pages

The Complete Project Manager's Toolkit
Randall Englund and Alfonso BuceroW

The Complete Project Manager's Toolkit will enable you to implement the easy-to-understand, universal, powerful, and immediately applicable concepts presented in *The Complete Project Manager*. You may already be aware of *what* you need to do; this book supplies the *how*.

Although *The Complete Project Manager's Toolkit* can be used as a stand-alone book, it is designed to complement *The Complete Project Manager: Integrating People, Organizational, and Technical Skills*.

ISBN 978-1-56726-360-2 ■ Product Code B602 ■ 203 pages

The Project Management Essential Library

The Project Management Essential Library is a series of eleven books, each of which covers a separate and distinct area of project management. The series provides project managers with new skills, clear explanations, and innovative approaches to the fundamentals of managing projects effectively. Whether further developing the skills you already have or adding tools to your repertoire, you will find insights in *The Project Management Essential Library* that you can immediately implement.

The Project Management Essential Library
Choose individual volumes ... or the complete library ...
And give your projects the best chance of success!

Six Sigma for Project Managers Steve Neuendorf ISBN 978-1-56726-146-2 Product Code B469	**Project Estimating and Cost Management** Parviz F. Rad, PhD, PMP ISBN 978-1-56726-144-8 ■ Product Code B442
The Triple Constraints in Project Management Michael S. Dobson, PMP ISBN 978-1-56726-152-3 Product Code B523	**Effective Work Breakdown Structures** Gregory T. Haugan, PhD, PMP ISBN 978-1-56726-135-6 ■ Product Code B353
Project Leadership Timothy J. Kloppenborg, PhD, PMP, Arthur Shriberg, EdD, and Jayashree Venkatraman ISBN 978-1-56726-145-5 ■ Product Code B450	**Project Planning and Scheduling** Gregory T. Haugan, PhD, PMP ISBN 978-1-56726-136-3 ■ Product Code B361
Managing Projects for Value John C. Goodpasture, PMP ISBN 978-1-56726-138-8 ■ Product Code B388	**Managing Project Quality** Timothy J. Kloppenborg, PhD, PMP, and Joseph A. Petrick, PhD ISBN 978-1-56726-141-7 ■ Product Code B418
Project Risk Management: A Proactive Approach Paul S. Royer, PMP ISBN 978-1-56726-139-4 ■ Product Code B396	**Managing Project Integration** Denis F. Cioffi, PhD ISBN 978-1-56726-134-9 ■ Product Code B345
Project Measurement Steve Neuendorf ISBN 978-1-56726-140-0 ■ Product Code B40X	**Full Set** Product Code B54X

Order today for a 30-day risk-free trial!
Visit www.managementconcepts.com/pubs or call 703-790-9595